Play Equipment
For Kids

Play Equipment For Kids

Great Projects You Can Build

Mike Lawrence

A Storey Publishing Book

STOREY

Storey Communications, Inc.
Schoolhouse Road
Pownal, Vermont 05261

The mission of Storey Communications is to serve our customers by publishing practical information that encourages personal independence in harmony with the environment.

United States edition published in 1996 by Storey Communications, Inc.,
Schoolhouse Road, Pownal, Vermont 05261
First published in 1994 by New Holland (Publishers) Ltd, 37 Connaught Street,
London W2 2AZ

The information in this book is true and complete to the best of our knowledge. All recommendations are made without guarantee on the part of the author or Storey Communications, Inc. The author and publisher disclaim any liability in connection with the use of this information. For additional information please contact Storey Communications, Inc., Schoolhouse Road, Pownal, Vermont 05261.

Co-ordination and picture research: Elizabeth Whiting & Associates
Editors: Coral Walker and John Boteler
U.S. editor: Gwen W. Steege
Consultants: Derek Bradford AJA RIBA and Penny Swift
Design: Cooper Wilson Design
Cover design: Cynthia McFarland
Cover photograph: ((TK))
U.S. production assistance: Michelle Arabia, Graphic Solutions
Illustration: Rob Shone
Originated by J Film Process, Singapore
Printed and bound in Malaysia by Times Offset (M) SDN BIID

Library of Congress Cataloging-in-Publication Data

Lawrence, Mike, 1947-
    Play equipment for kids : great projects you can build / Mike Lawrence.
       p.   cm.
    "A Storey publishing book."
    ISBN 0-88266-916-8
    1. Playgrounds—Equipment and supplies—Design and construction.
  2. Outdoor recreation—Equipment and supplies—Design and construction.
  3. Woodwork. I. Title.
TT176.L39   1996
    684.1'8—dc20   95-24038
                                                     CIP

The author would especially like to thank the following for their invaluable assistance: Stanley Tools for the loan of tools for special photograph, Met-Check, Milton Keynes for loan of instruments for the Weather Center Project and D.K.M. Design, London for special projects.

CONTENTS

INTRODUCTION

The great outdoors is every child's playground – or used to be in safer and more carefree times. Today, a private yard where your children can play to their heart's content is perhaps the greatest asset you can give them and, if you can include some stimulating and unusual play equipment, they will be even happier. In this book you will find ideas for play equipment of all types and for all ages. Make any – or all – of them and you will make their day!

Children are some of the greatest improvisers in the world. Their play activities often need only the simplest props; a cardboard box becomes a den, a few planks make an obstacle course and a hanging rope makes everyone a mini-Tarzan. They can suspend belief and make anything real, with a level of imagination and creativity that astonishes many adults. So whatever you build for them, do not be at all surprised if they quickly turn it into something completely different!

The importance of safety
The one thing children do not have – yet – is experience: experience with danger, with what is safe and sensible. It is here that the adult members of the family have the greatest responsibility for their care. Whatever we create for our children to play with must, as far as possible, use materials that will not harm them, structures that will stand up to boisterous wear and tear, and ground surfaces that will not injure them when they fall, as they inevitably will.

Much of this comes down to sensible design and careful planning. Wood is by far the most widely used material for all the projects in this book, and wood means splinters, unless corners are rounded off and the surfaces are finished smoothly. It also means that rot and insect attack is a

Left: *Trees are a natural source of fun for children; add an old tire and rope swing, but check the rope regularly for wear.*

slides; climbing frames and adventure playgrounds for the athletic; playhouses and cottages for the peacefully domesticated and forts and castles for the more belligerent.

Those perennial outdoor favorites, sand and water, are featured too, with plans for sandpits and pools that can become attractive planted gardens when the children grow up. And to conclude the book there are several smaller projects that can be put together in a day or a weekend, as the need arises. Many can even be built with the children's help – a factor that guarantees total acceptance by the players.

Building to scale

With many of the projects featured, it is important to keep a sense of scale to match the equipment to the ages and sizes of the children who will be using them. For

Left: *This 'play-center' was made by an artist. There are lots of ideas which could be incorporated into your own plans.*

Below: *A properly constructed playhouse of a generous size will be used throughout the year.*

long-term danger, so care must be taken at the planning stage to use preservative and decorative materials that are both long-lasting and safe. The need for good constructional techniques and adequate supports goes without saying.

The ground surfaces beneath play areas deserve attention too. Grass is the obvious first choice, but tends to wear badly as time goes by. Any hard surface – like concrete, or asphalt – is an obvious danger, and should be avoided. There are now

plenty of softer, safer alternatives available. You will find all these points covered in greater detail in the Reference section on pages 8-15.

Projects for all seasons

This book features play equipment of every sort, all easy to build from every-day materials – including recycled ones wherever possible – using only the simplest constructional techniques. There are traditional amusements such as swings, see-saws and

example, a climbing frame must have rungs that small hands can grip easily, and spaces between beams and rungs that small legs can reach without slipping dangerously between them. A swing needs only a narrow seat for a toddler, but a wider one for a larger child. Any building, whether a tree house or a castle, should be in scale with the size of its occupants if they are to feel at home in it. If adults cannot get inside, so much the better!

REFERENCE

There is more to building outdoor play equipment than simply fixing a few bits of wood together, especially if the resulting structure is to be safe to use, good to look at and, most important of all, appealing to your children. Before you start, you need to think about all the relevant factors in some detail, including where to place whatever you are building, how to make it as safe as possible for your children to use, how to integrate it into its surroundings, what raw materials and constructional techniques to use, how to cope with the question of maintenance and, if necessary, storage.

The obvious starting point for any project is in-depth consultation with the client – your children. You naturally hope to create something they will want to play with, so why not sit down at the beginning and ask them exactly what they have in mind? Remember that their imagination works on a completely different plane to yours, and your idea of a really challenging obstacle course or a perfect fairytale castle may be quite different to theirs.

Once you have agreed on a broad target for the project, it is your turn to think long and hard about all the other factors that are beyond a child's ability to perceive. Perhaps the most important of all is safety; what you build for them must take into consideration not only primary safety – obvious points such as equipment that cannot topple over in use – but also small but avoidable hazards such as surfaces that splinter in use or movable parts that could trap small hands and feet. Here are some points to ponder.

Primary safety
Many of the projects featured in this book involve three-dimensional structures into or on to which your children will climb. It is therefore vital that the structure is either stable enough in its own right not to topple over, even under the most extreme overloading – under 'birthday party' conditions, for example – or else is securely and permanently anchored to the ground or to some other appropriate means of support.

Play equipment such as climbing frames generally come into the former category. Here the aim is to devise a structure with a low center of gravity, so that even if every-one on it is hanging from one side, their weight will not pull it over. Wide bases and low heights are the answer.

Equipment like swings and see-saws comes into the second category. All need secure ground anchors, not only to resist movement of the apparatus itself but also to withstand infant terrorism: anything you fix they are sure to try to undo. For this reason, avoid solutions such as ground spikes which work loose and can be pulled out relatively easily unless they are at least 450 mm (18 in) long. If you are using ropes – to secure a tree house, for example – either use textbook knots which are self-tightening, or secure the ends with tamper-proof fittings. For fasteners to buildings and other structures, go for bolts with their positive locking action, rather than relying on nails which can pull out under weight. Above all, test all your fixings first under adult load conditions before entrusting them to your children.

This requirement also applies to the constructional techniques you use. Just because the structure is out of doors does not mean that it should not be well put together. Joints should be weatherproof and should interlock, and every component should be fitted to give a margin of safety in the event of over-loading or other misuse. You will find more detailed information on appropriate constructional techniques on page 14.

Surface safety
Once upon a time, civic playgrounds had concrete or asphalt surfaces which were inexpensive to lay, easy to maintain and relatively long-lasting. Unfortunately they were also extremely unforgiving if an accident occurred; a fall from a swing, an overshoot at the bottom of a slide or a spin off the merry-go-round would cause cuts and brush burns at best and broken bones at worst. Thankfully, the designers of public playgrounds have at last realized the dangers, helped in many countries by government legislation, and have begun to lay more user-friendly surfaces on to which falls mean bruises rather than fractures and smiles instead of tears.

Your grassy yard may be the safest possible site for a playground. However, in summer the sun can soon bake a lawn to the hardness of solid concrete. There are several other reasons why some people consider grass to be a less than suitable play surface. It can make a mess of children's clothes if wet and slippery: ask anyone who regularly has to wash them. It does not always wear well in constant use, leaving unsightly patches of bare earth where the endless passage of feet has torn out the grass roots; these then turn to mud whenever it rains. And if the grass does grow well, keeping it neat and tidy is made more difficult by the presence of the play equipment itself.

Professional playground designers now use a range of synthetic ground surfaces that provide some cushioning to prevent serious injury. Unfortunately these are not generally available to the amateur, who must therefore improvise an alternative solution. One possibility is to place play equipment in an area covered with a generous bed of chipped bark or similar organic material which is relatively inert and provides the necessary soft landing. Fine washed river sand is an option worth considering if you fear that bark chippings are likely to be blown around by the prevailing winds, but soil is not. It will be picked up on hands and feet, may stain clothing and will become a quagmire in wet weather. Whichever material you use should be laid to a depth of at least 150 mm (6 in) over a fast-draining sub-base, and the area should be contained by some form of perimeter restraint such as pegged boards or path edging stones.

Secondary safety
So far so good: with some careful planning and design, what you are intending to build will be strong enough to do its job, secure enough to be safe in use and placed on a surface that will not injure or maim.

Right: *Play structures need not be expensive. Before deciding what to build, check what recyclable materials you have around.*

You now need to think about safety on a smaller scale, by paying attention to all those little details that make the difference between a safe play area and one that causes a series of troublesome and avoidable accidents and injuries.

Since wood is the first choice material for so many of the projects in this book, careful selection and high-quality finishing are vitally important. The wood you use should wherever possible be free from defects such as splits and cracks for maximum strength and durability. Try to avoid wood with a lot of knots too, since these can weaken the wood and will leave potentially dangerous holes and rough edges if they shrink and fall out. If you are using second-hand wood (see Materials for more information) take special care to ensure that it does not contain any old rusty nails or screws that could cause injury.

As for finishes, the main object of the exercise is to avoid the risk of splinters. This means rounding off all square-cut corners and edges which can soon become split in use, and giving all flat surfaces a reasonably smooth finish.

Take care too to ensure that all fasteners are recessed into the wood so they cannot cause injuries. This means countersinking screw heads and nail heads (and checking that their points do not protrude anywhere) and recessing bolt heads and threaded tails plus their nuts in counterbores (deep countersunk holes). These should all be rustproof wherever possible.

Whatever you are constructing, keep an eye open for finger traps – crevices and other narrow gaps in the structure that could pinch or trap a child's fingers. This point is especially important on play equipment with moving parts. Remember that a child's hand can easily slip in where an adult's could not.

Lastly, think carefully about the safety aspect of any decorative or protective treatment you give to your play equipment. Try to avoid toxic chemicals, and treat any rust-prone metallic components with lead-free, rust-inhibiting paint unless they are galvanized, and therefore rust-proof.

Sand and water

Sand in sandpits introduces another safety angle. For a start, the sand should be washed concreting or river sand rather than soft bricklaying sand, which can stain skin and clothing. Sandpits always appeal to pets – especially cats and dogs – as convenient toilets, posing an obvious danger of infection from urine and fecal matter buried in the sand. To discourage their visits, always cover sandpits when

they are not in use, either with a tarp or similar sheet or with a rigid cover made from exterior-quality plywood or corrugated plastic sheeting.

If you have small children and a wading pool, it pays to be aware of the dangers of water; an unsupervised child can drown in minutes in only a few inches of water. To avoid accidents, the safest solution is either to install a rigid cover as recommended for a sandbox, or else to empty the pool with a siphon or small pump whenever it is not in use.

Blending with the background

Integrating play equipment with its surroundings is also an important factor. For a start, bright primary colors may look well in a public playground, but are unlikely to suit a private yard where restful, natural colors will be more in keeping with the setting.

Where you place play equipment is also important. Naturally, you will want to keep an eye on small children, so placing their equipment fairly near the house is sensible. Since this is likely to be on a relatively small scale, you may find it preferable to move it out into view when it is needed, and to store it out of sight otherwise.

Play equipment for older children – especially more permanent structures such as tree houses, climbing frames and adventure playgrounds – can be placed further away from the house if the yard size and layout allows; they much prefer to be as far as possible from adult supervision. Try to use existing yard features such as mature trees and dividing screens to camouflage the equipment, and do not be afraid to introduce new plantings if necessary to soften its appearance.

Materials

Most pressure-treated wood is impregnated with inorganic arsenic to protect it against damage by insects and fungi. Although some argue that this wood is safe after a period of time, others recommend against using it on surfaces that children may touch. Instead of using pressure-treated wood, you may choose to treat natural soft- or hardwoods with copper napthenate or sodium borate, which help prevent insect damage, and a water repellent, to keep wood from absorbing water.

You can use sawed timber for elements of the structure that will not be climbed, sat on or otherwise handled, but it is wise to select planed timber (finished lumber) otherwise to help eliminate the risk of splinters.

If what you are constructing requires the use of synthetic boards, the best to use

is exterior-grade medium-density fiberboard or, if weight is no problem, roofing-grade particle board). Exterior-grade plywood is relatively expensive and is prone to edge splintering unless very carefully finished.

Recycled materials – especially timber – will make any structure you build cheaper, but also such wood will generally be well seasoned and may also be attractively weathered, helping the structures to blend in more naturally with their surroundings. However, care must be taken to ensure that any second-hand wood you use is sound, free from rot and insect attack and, above all, has been carefully examined to ensure that it does not contain any old, rusty fasteners that could cause injury.

Concrete

For several of the projects featured in this book, you will be using small quantities of concrete to secure posts in the ground. Use a 1:2:3 cement:sand:aggregate mix, made with coarse 20mm (¾ in) aggregate. If you are using combined aggregates, use a 1:5 mix. As a guide; a 50 kg (110 lb) bag of cement mixed with aggregate will yield 0.15 cu m (6 cu ft) of concrete.

The essential tool kit

Even if your construction activities are relatively limited, you will not achieve very good results without using the right tools and equipment. Here is a guide to some of the tools you will certainly need, and others you may want to add to your tool kit.

Basic fasteners

Perhaps the simplest of all do-it-yourself jobs is assembling things. In each case you have to make a fastener of some sort – either driving a nail or a screw, or fastening a nut and bolt. Nails are easier to use than screws; all you need to drive them is a hammer (see below). However, they can pull out suddenly if they are subjected to a heavy load. Screws are better: they provide a more secure grip, and can be undone relatively easily if you want to move or change the fastener. The only trouble is that you need separate tools to make the hole and to drive the screw. Better still for some constructions are nuts and bolts; use them where strength and rigidity are essential, or when you want to be able to dismantle what you have built.

Drills

As far as tools are concerned, requirement number one is a drill. These days there is little point in buying a hand drill such as your grandfather used. Instead, invest in an electric drill, ideally one with a 13 mm (½ in) chuck, variable speed control and hammer action, so you can tackle a wide range of drilling jobs in all sorts of materials with just the one tool. Cordless types are ideal for outdoor use, but they do need regular recharging.

If you prefer to use a mains-powered tool, you will also need an extension cord so you can use your drill away from an indoor power source. Buy one that is flexible and insulated rated at 13 or 15 amps (depending on the system used) rather than 5 amps, so you can use it for running more powerful equipment such as heaters too, when you are not using it for do-it-yourself jobs.

For actually making the holes, you will need a variety of drill bits. Buy high-speed steel twist drill bits for making holes in wood, plus two or three masonry drill bits for making holes in walls. Twist drill bits are sized in millimetres or in fractions of an inch, and are sold in sets as well as singly. The maximum size hole you can drill with them is about 13 mm (½ in) in diameter. For making larger holes in wood, you can buy spade-shaped wood bits in sizes up to about 38 mm (1½ in). Masonry drills are sized either by numbers that match screw gauges, or in millimetres.

Screwdrivers
For driving screws you need a screwdriver. To be precise, you need several screwdrivers, because screws come in several sizes and have heads of different types. For the driver to work efficiently, its blade must match the slot or recess in the screw head. If it slips out, it will damage the screw and also whatever you are fixing. You can probably get by with just two flat-bladed screwdrivers of different sizes for driving slotted screws, plus one or two cross-point drivers for cross-head (Philips) screws. Pozidriv and Supadriv are the commonest types; a No 2 size screwdriver will drive the most widely-used screw sizes. Most screwdrivers have plastic handles; choose ones that feel comfortable in your hand.

As an alternative, you can use power tools to drive screws; either fit screw-driver bits in a variable-speed drill, or use a cordless screwdriver.

Measuring and marking tools
There are a couple of other tools you will find invaluable when you are putting things together. The first is a retractable steel measuring tape. Choose one with a tape at least 3 m (10 ft) long, preferably with both metric and imperial measurements; it is a good idea to choose one with a lock so you can take long measurements without the

tape coiling up unexpectedly. The second tool is a small spirit level, invaluable for ensuring that you fix things to a true horizontal. Choose one at least 600 mm (2 ft) long with a metal body and horizontal and vertical indicators; then you can use it as a straightedge too. Add a pencil, for marking the positions of fastening holes and joints, drawing cutting lines and so on.

Hammers
Despite what was said earlier about the superiority of screws for making secure fastenings, a hammer is a tool no one should be without. Choose a claw hammer, which can pull nails out as well as drive them. The best will have a moulded rubber handgrip and a metal, fiberglass or wooden shaft.

A trimming knife
There are all sorts of jobs where a sharp knife is invaluable. Choose a trimming knife with a retractable blade, so you can carry it around safely, and buy a selection of blades for it, including ordinary cutting blades and a padsaw (utility knife) blade for making small cut-outs in wood and other materials.

Saws
Even if you plan to do no more carpentry than cutting a few planks to length, you must have a saw. A tenon saw will cope with most small sawing jobs on thin man-

Above: *The sandpit and swing blend in well with the existing garden, and it is also possible to keep an eye on the children.*

made boards and on timber up to about 50 mm (2 in) thick. Choose one with a 300 mm or 350 mm (12 in to 14 in) blade and a plastic or good-quality wooden handle. Invest in a try square (set square) too, so you can make sure your saw cuts are absolutely square. Use a panel or log saw for cutting thicker wood.

If you prefer, buy an electric jig (scrolling) saw. This is an extremely versatile tool which can cut straight lines, curves and other intricate cutouts in a wide variety of materials up to about 65 mm (2½ in) thick. Choose a saw with variable speed control, so you can use a low speed for hard materials and a high speed for softer ones. There are different types of blades for cutting natural timber and man-made boards. As with power drills, cordless types of jig saw are available that are ideal for outdoor use.

A planer file
If you are working with wood, there are likely to be a variety of shaping jobs you will have to tackle. A Surform, which is a general purpose plane/rasp, is ideal for working with both wood and man-made boards, and can tackle metal too. Surforms come in a range of styles, including flat

rasps, planer-files, round files and block planes. All have replaceable blades.

A small hacksaw

You are likely to have to tackle some small metal-cutting jobs, especially away from the workbench. Examples include cutting through rusty screws and bolts and cutting metal pipes to length. A small hacksaw takes cheap, throwaway blades which are simply snapped into place in the frame; choose one with a comfortable handle.

Adjustable wrenches

You are likely to be using nuts and bolts of various types that need tightening or loosening. In an ideal world you would have a different wrench for every nut, but for the time being a couple of adjustable (shifting) wrenches will come in very handy (you need two because often you will have to grip a nut as well as a bolt). Choose one small and one medium wrench, to cope with a wide range of nut and bolt sizes.

A pair of pliers

Pliers are a real jack-of-all-trades tool – they will grip all sorts of things you may be trying to undo or tighten up, bend things like stiff wire or metal sheets and so on. Choose a pair of combination pliers with fine and coarse serrated jaws and a wire cutter near the pivot point; plastic hand grips make them more comfortable to use.

A portable workbench

A portable workbench is a must. Not only can you take it to wherever you want and provide a firm, stable surface on which to work, you can also use it as a vice for gripping things, and you can even stand on it and use it as a makeshift working platform.

Tools you may also need

What other woodworking tools you need-depends on the scale of the projects you will be tackling, and on whether you want to use traditional hand tools wherever possible, or prefer to put your faith as much as possible in modern power tools.

For general cutting work beyond the capacity of your tenon saw or power jig saw you will need a panel saw, a log saw or a circular saw (skilsaw). A circular saw can be used freehand, but is more versatile if used in conjunction with a saw table. For curved cuts you will need a coping saw.

For reducing wood to the cross-section you require, you will need either a smoothing plane or an electric power planer. You can shape it using traditional hand tools such as rasps or files and drawknives, or let power tools do the work for you; you could use a belt sander for fast stock removal, plus a range of drill attachments such as drum sanders and rotary wood rasps to do the finer shaping work.

When it comes to cutting joints, a set of wood chisels is essential, whether you prefer hand or power tools for other jobs. Bevel-edge chisels are more versatile than firmer chisels because you can undercut with them; you need at least four, in 6 mm, 12 mm, 18 mm and 25 mm (¼ in, ½ in, ¾ in and 1 in) widths. You will also need an oilstone to keep them sharp.

Talking of hammers, it is worth adding a small tack hammer to your tool kit, for driving small nails and tacks. A heavy-duty staple gun is also worth having, since it allows you to make instant fasteners of thin sheet materials and fabrics with one hand free to position the work while the other fires the staples.

For making holes in wood, the power drill reigns supreme. You can fit drill bits of all sorts into it for making large and small

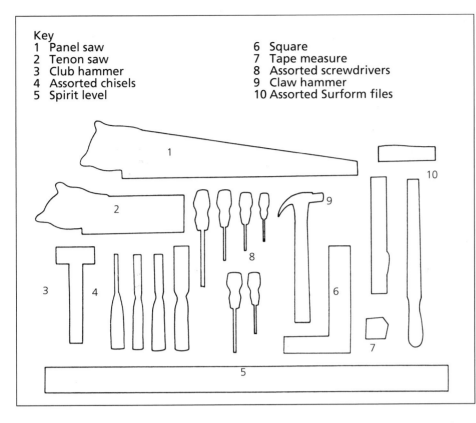

Key
1 Panel saw
2 Tenon saw
3 Club hammer
4 Assorted chisels
5 Spirit level
6 Square
7 Tape measure
8 Assorted screwdrivers
9 Claw hammer
10 Assorted Surform files

holes, and with a hole saw attachment you can cut even larger holes in sheet materials. A vertical drill stand is a useful accessory if you do a lot of drilling, since it ensures that holes are drilled precisely vertically and, if necessary, to just the right depth.

For assembling the fruits of your labors, some clamps will be invaluable. There are many different patterns on the market; add them to your tool kit as you find you need them. Remember that you can use your portable workbench as a vice.

A countersink bit for your power drill enables you to recess screw heads below the wood surface; a nail set lets you recess nail heads. Lastly, it will pay you to expand your selection of screwdrivers, both flat-bladed and cross-point (Phillips) types. If you have a lot of repetitive driving to do,

invest in either a spiral ratchet screwdriver or a cordless power screwdriver; both come with a range of interchangeable bits.

The last stage in any project is the final finishing. You can do this either by hand with abrasive paper and a sanding block, or else invest in a powered orbital sander.

Construction techniques

For the sort of projects described in this book, strength and rigidity are more important than subtlety. So most of the joints you use to put things together are likely to be simple butt joints that rely on a fastening device – nails, screws or nuts and bolts – to hold the components securely together.

The one drawback with this type of joint is that unless two or more fastenings

are used per joint, there is always a tendency for the joint to rotate out of position under weight. It is better if possible to introduce some degree of physical interlocking between the two joint components, and the simple lap joint is one way of doing this without the need for any intricate joint-cutting.

The corner lap joint is the simplest of the family, and is used as its name suggests to form an L-shaped joint at the corner of a two-dimensional frame. It can be cut with just a tenon saw on all but relatively thick wood. Half the thickness of each component is cut away, so that when the joint is assembled the shoulders of the joint interlock and so help to prevent any rotation from taking place. Another advantage over a simple butt joint is that the two components are now in the same plane, making it easy to attach clapboard materials to the frame.

The tee-lap and cross-lap joints are variations on the same theme. In a tee-lap joint one component – the stem of the tee – is prepared in the same way as for a corner lap joint. The other component has half its thickness removed at the joint position, a job that requires a chisel as well as a tenon saw to remove the waste wood. The cross-lap joint has both components prepared as for the cross piece of a tee-lap joint, allowing them to interlock to form a rigid cross shape.

All lap joints are best assembled with woodworking adhesive – a waterproof type, naturally, for outdoor use – and can be given additional reinforcement with nails, screws or nuts and bolts.

There is seldom a need to use any other more elaborate woodworking joints on the sort of projects featured in this book, with the possible exception of the lap joint for linking horizontal rails to a vertical post. Where the rails are much thinner than the post cross-section, a full-lap joint can be used. Here adjacent sides of the post are

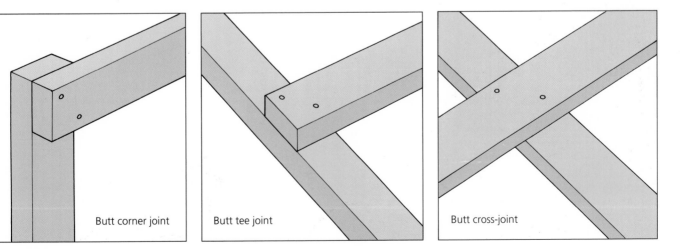

Butt corner joint

Butt tee joint

Butt cross-joint

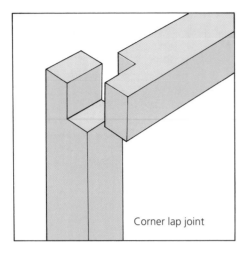

Corner lap joint

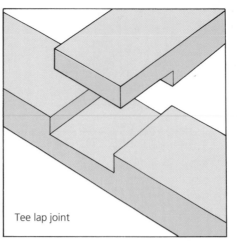

Tee lap joint

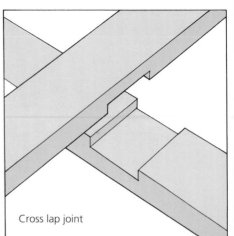

Cross lap joint

cut away in a step shape to match the rail thickness, so providing a ledge on which the rail is supported. If cutting the joint in this way would leave an unacceptably small stub at the top of the post, the half-lap joint is used instead. Here the ends of the rails are cut down to half their thickness, as in a corner lap joint, and a correspondingly narrow step is cut in the face of the post. The ends of the rails can be butt-jointed or mitered.

Several of the projects in the book feature ladders formed by setting round softwood rungs between horizontal or vertical rungs. Here the rungs are simply glued and pinned into matching holes drilled in the rungs with a wood bit or hole saw of the appropriate diameter.

Ground anchors

The best way of securing play equipment to the ground is to bury its main support posts in the ground and surround it with concrete, in much the same way as you would put up a fence post. This is especially recommended for equipment such as swings and climbing frames, where there are sizeable lateral forces acting on the structure. Where concreting is not suitable or appropriate, an alternative is to use long

metal spikes which are driven deep into the ground with a sledgehammer, and which are hooked over the ground-level components of the structure to anchor it firmly in place. Such spikes should be a minimum of 450 mm (18 in) long and at least 10 mm (⅜ in) in diameter; anything smaller could gradually work free and be pulled out of the ground as time goes by.

Maintenance

It is vital from the safety point of view that any outdoor play structure is well main-

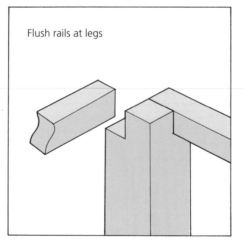

Flush rails at legs

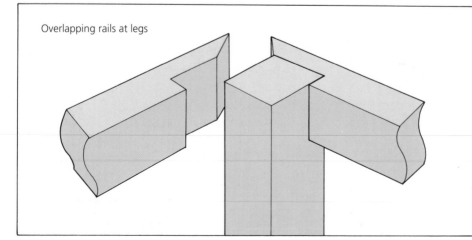

Overlapping rails at legs

tained. This means inspecting it at regular intervals for any signs of wear – loose joints, damaged components, insecure fasteners, splintered surfaces and so on. If any faults are found, the equipment must either be repaired immediately or taken out of commission until the necessary repairs can be carried out.

With wooden structures, look especially carefully for any evidence of rot or insect attack. Both are likely to attack at (or below) ground level, and at joints where end-grain is exposed. Any affected wood must be cut out immediately and replaced with sound new wood.

From the general maintenance point of view, wood should be given a fresh coat of preservative (see page 10) every year, following a careful inspection of the structure. A water-repellent oil coating should be recoated every six months at first. Avoid using paint if possible, since it can obscure rot and other faults. Treat rust on fasteners with a proprietary rust remover, or paint over them with a rust-inhibiting paint.

Storage

Unless you are building structures that will be a permanent part of the landscape, you need to give some consideration to the question of storage. Except for smaller items, this means designing things so they can be partially dismantled relatively quickly and easily; using wing nuts and bolts for the separate sections is one possible solution to this problem.

As far as storage is concerned, make use of any covered space you may have, otherwise, stack the equipment off the ground, and cover it with securely-tied tarpaulins or other waterproof covers. Avoid thin polyethylene sheeting, which can soon be torn to shreds by strong winds.

Below: *Make sure climbing frames, etc. are sturdy enough, check regularly for any problems, and mend immediately.*

SWINGS, SEE-SAWS AND SLIDES

Perhaps the most traditional of all items of play equipment are the trio that dominate playgrounds the world over: the swing, the see-saw and the slide. All operate on the simplest of physical principles – what goes up must come down – but each offers its own range of special sensations. Each can be constructed in a variety of different ways, on a scale to suit the children who will be using them, but in every case safety is paramount. Swings and see-saws need the strength to withstand being pushed to their limits, while slides must guarantee a safe landing.

The swing in particular exerts a strange fascination for children, enabling them to experience the exhilarating yet stomach-churning sensations that abrupt changes of direction cause as they swing higher and higher. Because of the way a swing works, it needs the sturdiest possible construction; the forces imposed on it as the swinger swoops backwards and forwards can be very high, both on the chains or ropes suspending the seat and on the structure of the swing's framework. With a typical A-shaped frame, each arc of the swing tends to lift the opposite side of the frame off the ground, while a swing set in an arch simply pulls the vertical arch supports alternately forwards and backwards as the swing oscillates. The securest possible ground anchors are therefore essential.

In the case of an arch frame, the best solution is to set the vertical supports in the ground, embedded in concrete, in much the same way as you would fix a fence post. With A-shaped frames, long metal ground spikes driven in at an angle to oppose the lifting forces are the answer, but even these can work loose in time if the swing is vigorously used, and regular inspection of the anchors' security is therefore essential. If such spikes are not readily available, an engineering firm might make them up for you.

It is also a good idea to give some thought to seat safety. For very young children

Left: *Older children will enjoy the challenge of these 'professional' rings.*

Below: *An old-fashioned swing will give enjoyment to children and adults alike, especially in such a tranquil setting.*

Above: *Falls from this rope ladder and swing are cushioned by plenty of straw.*

it is important to provide a chair seat with some sort of lap safety bar, while for older children a simple plank seat will usually suffice. However, many accidents are caused by collisions between freely-swinging seats and unwary children's heads, so padding the edges of swing seats is a sensible precaution. Alternatively, an old car tire can be partly cut away and adapted to form a very safe seat for young children – but clean it thoroughly first.

Lastly, the seat supports must be strong enough for their job and must also be securely attached both to the swing sup-

ports and to the seat. Welded-link galvanized steel chain is the most durable support, and can be bought from specialist chain manufacturers complete with the necessary mounting eyebolts and nuts. Alternatively, you can use strong nylon or polypropylene rope, which is available complete with the necessary fastener cleats from sailboat dealers and some specialist hardware suppliers.

See-saws of the type seen in public playgrounds are usually spring-operated – a mechanism you cannot easily replicate in your yard. It is therefore best to restrict

home-made see-saws to small gravity-operated types suitable just for toddlers – see page 26 for details.

Slides can be free-standing or, if the yard has a steep slope, can be built into a bank. The former can easily be made on a small scale – see page 28 for more details – but can be difficult to construct on a playground scale because of the obvious safety risks.

SIMPLE ARCH SWING

The earliest rope swings were probably hung from the branch of a tree, and an arch swing suspended from a horizontal beam is the nearest man-made equivalent. This is one of the easiest structures to build. For safety, the uprights must be set in concrete.

Materials
Hardcore
Concrete

Swing: from planed softwood
2 x 3 m x 100 mm x 100 mm (10 ft x 4 in x 4 in) uprights
1 x 1 m x 100 mm x 100 mm (3 ft x 4 in x 4 in) crossbar
4 x 150 mm x 50 mm (6 in x 2 in) narrow support strips
Eyebolts
Nuts
Nails
Long screws
Rope/swing chain
Nylon rope clamps/chain shackles

Seat: from planed softwood
2 x 550 mm x 100 mm x 25 mm (22 in x 4 in x 1 in) slats
2 x 300 mm x 100 mm x 25 mm (12 in x 4 in x 1 in) support blocks
Foam rubber
Vinyl upholstery fabric
Heavy-duty staples

The beam can be part of an existing yard structure, or you can build a simple free-standing arch consisting of two vertical supports bridged by a horizontal cross-piece. You can even incorporate it in a more elaborate structure such as a pergola if you wish.

This is without doubt the easiest type of swing to construct, since all you need are the two uprights spaced a reasonable distance – say 1 m (just over 3 ft) – apart, and a well-secured beam spanning their tops to form a sturdy support for the swing itself.

To ensure that the structure can withstand the lateral forces that will be imposed on it, the uprights must be set in the ground and secured with concrete.

The crossbar must be thick enough to cope with potential overloading – swing seats often have more than one occupant! If you follow the dimensions and step-by-

step instructions given here, the end result will be a sturdy swing that will give your children hours of pleasure.

Cutting the components
The dimensions given are for a standard-sized swing, but you can scale them down if you wish to make a swing suitable for smaller children.

The two uprights are cut from planed softwood. (You can use narrower boards – 76 mm x 76 mm [3 in x 3 in] – it will work just as well.) They must be long enough to allow for about 900 mm (3 ft) of their length to be embedded in the ground. The crossbar is cut from the same square wood, and rests on top of the two uprights. It is secured to them by narrow strips of wood that are screwed to each side of the cross-

Above: It is important to position swings where other children will not be in danger of being hit.

bar and to the sides of the uprights to form a strong support for the swing. Two large eyebolts screwed through holes in the crossbar provide supports for the seat ropes or chains.

The seat is made up by screwing the two 550 mm (22 in) lengths of softwood to the two shorter support blocks of the same-sized wood. The seat and the support blocks are drilled at each side of the seat to provide secure fasteners for the supporting ropes or chains, which can either pass through to the underside of the seat or can be attached to eyebolts.

4 Drill two holes about 500 mm (20 in) apart in the crossbar and attach the eye-bolts for the seat support ropes. Tighten the nuts fully so the bolts are secure.

5 Attach the seat support ropes or chains to the eyebolts, ready for the seat to be attached. Use manufactured chain shackles or special nylon rope clamps to make the fasteners, and test that they are secure.

Making a simple slat seat

6 Glue and screw the timber components together. Drill holes for the support rope – or for eyebolts if you are using chain – through the seat and the support blocks, about 25 mm (1 in) in from the seat corners.

7 Pass rope down through one hole, across the underside of the support block and

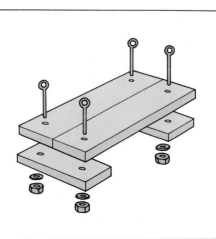

1

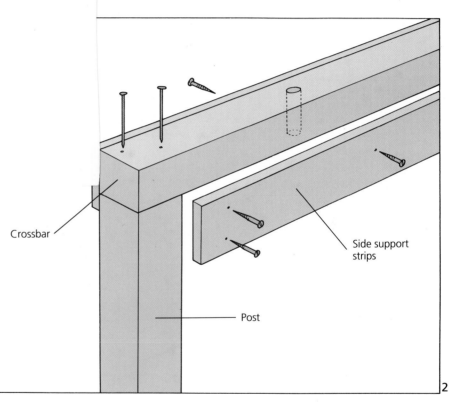

Crossbar

Side support strips

Post

2

Making the swing

1 Excavate two 300 mm (12 in) square holes about 1 m (3 ft 3 in) apart to a depth of 900 mm (3 ft) to take the uprights. Set each one in its hole, brace it upright and check that it is level with its neighbour. Ram in broken bricks around the base and add concrete to each one. Smooth off the concrete and leave it to harden for 48-72 hours (see diagram 1).

2 Nail the crossbar to the tops of the posts. Then add the two narrow support strips, with their top edges level with its upper surface (diagram 2).

3 Drive long screws through the outer face of each strip into both the crossbar and the uprights to secure the crossbar in place.

back up through the other hole, securing the cut end to the main length of rope with a clamp.

8 Attach eyebolts for the support chains (diagram 3), tightening the nuts before attaching the chain with shackles.

Safety first

Seats of this type can cause a bad injury if they strike a child. You can soften the edges by gluing on pieces of dense under-padding. Cover the seat with a piece of vinyl upholstery fabric, pull it taut across the seat and over the foam and staple it to the underside of the seat.

3

Crossbar

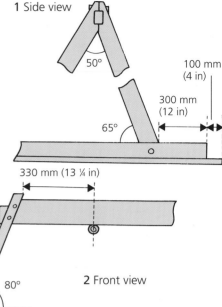

1 Side view

50°

65°

80°

2 Front view

100 mm (4 in)

300 mm (12 in)

330 mm (13 ¼ in)

Seat

Leg

Sideplate

Ground board

A FRAME SWING

The traditional swing – the A-frame – is a sturdy and stable structure. This design can be adapted to suit children of all ages. A plank seat is perfectly adequate for older children, while younger ones can be provided with a chair seat.

Materials
Frame: from preservative-treated planed softwood
4 x 2.7 m x 76 mm x 50 mm (8 ft 10 in x 3 in x 2 in) legs
1 x 1.825 m x 100 mm x 76 mm (6 ft 4 in x 3 in) crossbar
2 x 2.9 m x 50 mm x 25 mm (9 ft 6 in x 2 in x 1 in) side plates
2 x 3.1 m x 76 mm x 25 mm (10 ft 2 in x 3 in x 1 in) ground boards

75 mm (3 in) carriage bolts
125 mm (5 in) carriage bolts
Eyebolts to attach rope/chain to seat
Corresponding nuts and locking washers
Screws
Woodworking adhesive
Rope/swing chain

Panel seat for older children:
1 x 500 mm x 175 mm x 25 mm (20 in x 7 in x 1 in) timber seat board
2 x 500 mm x 25 mm x 25 mm (20 in x 1 in x 1 in) narrow strips to edge seat
2 x 175 mm x 25 mm x 25 mm (7 in x 1 in x 1 in) narrow strips to edge seat
50 mm (2 in) diameter half-round chip foam
Panel pins
Strong all-purpose adhesive
Vinyl upholstery fabric
Heavy-duty staples

Chair seat for smaller child:
From exterior-quality 25 mm (1 in) thick plywood

1 x 510 mm x 430 mm (20 in x 17 in) top/arm rest
1 x 400 mm x 330 mm (15¾ in x 13 in) seat
1 x 310 mm x 200 mm (12¼ in x 8 in) back
2 x 310 mm x 100 mm (12¼ in x 4 in) sides
9 mm (⅜ in) dowel rod
Woodworking adhesive
Chip foam
Strong all-purpose adhesive
Vinyl upholstery fabric
Screws
Leather strap (optional)

If you do not want to build an in-ground arch swing (pages 18-19), the strongest and most stable alternative is to make one with a traditional A-frame design. The two side frames provide a wide base that resists toppling even when the seat swings high, as well as supporting a sturdy crossbar from which the seat is suspended.

Since the only link between the two A-frames is the crossbar, it is essential either that the ground boards are fixed down with long metal ground anchors or that cross beams are fitted at ground level to link the ends of the frames together.

The dimensions given below are for a standard-sized swing, but you can scale the construction down for smaller children.

You can make the swing with a simple plank seat or, for smaller children, a chair seat with lap strap. In either case you can adjust the height of the seat to suit the ages of the children who will be using it.

Cutting the components
Use planed wood for making the swing and the basic seat. If you decide to make the chair seat, you will need some 25 mm (1 in) thick exterior-quality plywood as well.

In the materials list, use only the metric measurements for complete accuracy; the imperial measurements are given only as an *approximate* conversion. If the sizes quoted are not available, rip or plane larger stock down to the sizes given.

Preparing the crossbar
Start by cutting the crossbar to length. You will see from the diagrams (3 and 4 overleaf) that a shouldered tenon is formed on each end, and that this is bolted into matching cut-outs formed in the tops of each of the legs.

Left: *This A-frame swing needs a generous amount of clear, flat space. It is obviously an advantage to be able to move it around.*

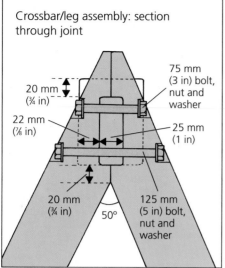

Crossbar/leg assembly: section through joint

20 mm (¾ in)

75 mm (3 in) bolt, nut and washer

22 mm (⅞ in)

25 mm (1 in)

20 mm (¾ in)

125 mm (5 in) bolt, nut and washer

50°

3

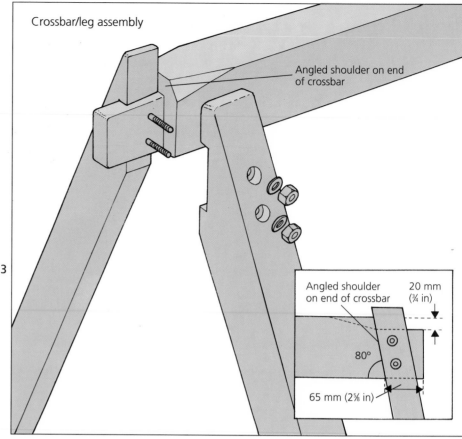

Crossbar/leg assembly

Angled shoulder on end of crossbar

Angled shoulder on end of crossbar

20 mm (¾ in)

80°

65 mm (2⅝ in)

4

1 First mark points on the lower edge of the crossbar, each 65 mm (2½ in) in from the end. Then use a protractor to set a sliding bevel to an angle of 80° and draw a line across the side of the crossbar through each of the two marks. This line represents the angle that will be formed between the legs and the crossbar when the swing is assembled.

2 Next, draw a line on the side of the crossbar at each end, parallel with the top edge and 20 mm (¾ in) below it. This intersects with the 80°-angled line to mark the area of waste wood which must be removed to form the shoulder of the tenon.

3 Once you have formed this shoulder with your saw, use a mortise or marking gauge to mark a tenon 25 mm (1 in) wide on the center of each end of the crossbar, as shown in diagram 4, and cut away the waste wood carefully to leave a tenon with an angled shoulder, ready to be bolted in place between the matching shaped cut-outs in the legs.

Assembling the frame
4 Cut the four legs to length. Then use your protractor and sliding bevel to mark the cutting angles on each end of each leg. The bottom of each leg is cut to an angle of 65° (diagram 1), while at the top a cut is made at an angle of 25° to the edge of each leg, allowing each pair to meet with an angle of 50° between them (diagram 3).

5 Hold the angled top edge of each leg against the side of the crossbar tenon with its side face pressed against the angled shoulder of the tenon.

6 Mark the outline of the tenon on the angled edge of the leg, and then extend the marked lines onto the side faces of the legs so you can mark a cut-out approximately 13 mm (½ in) deep.

7 Use a tenon saw and chisel to remove the waste wood. (When each pair of legs is brought together, these cut-outs will form a mortise around the tenon on each end of the crossbar.)

8 Check the fit of the joints. Then clamp each pair of legs to the crossbar and drill two 10 mm (⅜ in) holes through the legs and the crossbar tenon as shown in diagram 3.

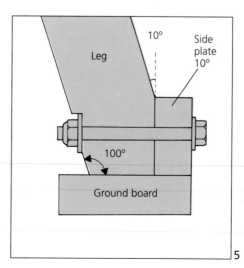

10°

Side plate 10°

Leg

100°

Ground board

5

9 Counter-bore all the holes to a diameter of 25 mm (1 in) and a depth of 15 mm (¾ in), and bolt the joints together using a 75 mm (3 in) long M10 carriage bolt through the upper holes and a 125 mm (5 in) bolt through the lower ones. Use locking washers beneath the nuts so that they cannot work loose.

Adding the side plates and ground boards
10 You have already angled the bottom ends of the frame legs to 65°. Now use your protractor and sliding bevel again, this time to draw a line across the bottom face of each leg at an angle of 100°, as shown in diagram 5, to allow the angled leg to stand flat on the ground board.

11 Cut the bottom of each leg to the marked angle. Then cut off the outer edge of each leg at right angles to the 100° line so that the side plates can be fitted at right angles to the ground boards; see the cross-sectional diagram 5 again for clarification of this step.

12 Now you can glue and screw the side plates to the ground boards, stand the swing frame on the completed side plate/ground board assemblies and drill a 10 mm (⅜ in) diameter bolt hole through the side plate into the center of each leg.

Right: A chair seat would be more suitable for smaller children. For extra safety, fit a strap or length of rope as a lap restraint.

Bolt the plate to the leg with a 75 mm (3 in) long bolt, nut and locking washer. That completes the swing frame.

Making the panel seat

13 Drill a 10 mm (⅜ in) diameter hole through the 500 mm (20 in) board at each side, 50 mm (2 in) in from the ends, to take the support rope/chain (diagram 6).

14 Thicken the edges of the board by gluing and pinning on the softwood strips all round. Glue pieces of half-round chip-foam to the front and rear edges of the seat for comfort and protection from accidents.

15 Complete the seat by stapling on a piece of vinyl upholstery fabric, turning it over the foam edges on to the underside. Pierce the fabric over the bolt hole positions and fit the bolts with nuts and washers ready for the support ropes/chains.

Making the chair seat

1 Mark and cut out the components from the plywood using the dimensions and the cut-outs shown in the diagram. Save the piece cut off from the top/armrest section to make a drop-in seat (see diagram 7).

2 Make the various cut-outs as shown, then test-fit the back and sides into them.

3 Drill holes for the dowels as shown, and assemble the seat by gluing and dowelling all the components together.

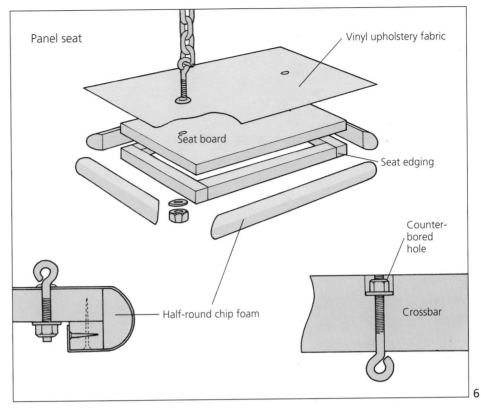

Panel seat · Vinyl upholstery fabric · Seat board · Seat edging · Counter-bored hole · Half-round chip foam · Crossbar

6

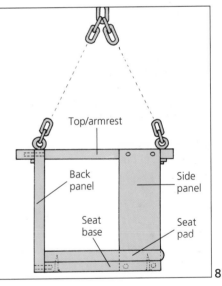

Top/armrest · Back panel · Side panel · Seat base · Seat pad

8

4 Drill four holes as shown for the eyebolts, fit them with washers and nuts and attach the support ropes/chains (diagram 8).

5 Complete the chair by making the drop-in seat section. Glue some chip-foam to the front edge of the plywood piece you saved earlier, cover it with a stapled-on piece of vinyl upholstery fabric and secure the drop-in section by driving screws up through the chair seat into it.

6 For complete safety, fit a leather strap or a length of rope with clip-on shackles and attach it to the front two eyebolts to form a lap restraint.

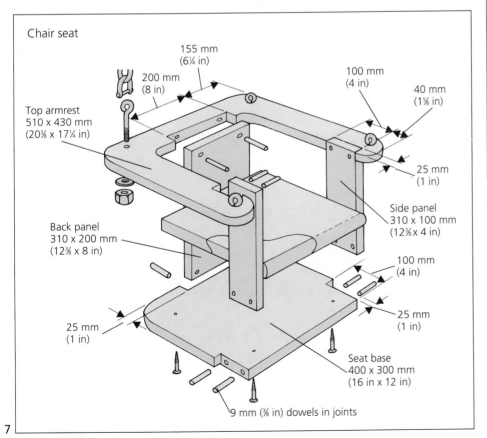

Chair seat

155 mm (6¼ in)
200 mm (8 in)
100 mm (4 in)
40 mm (1⅝ in)

Top armrest 510 x 430 mm (20⅜ x 17¼ in)

Back panel 310 x 200 mm (12⅜ x 8 in)

25 mm (1 in)

Side panel 310 x 100 mm (12⅜ x 4 in)

25 mm (1 in)

100 mm (4 in)

25 mm (1 in)

Seat base 400 x 300 mm (16 in x 12 in)

9 mm (⅜ in) dowels in joints

7

RUSTIC ARCH SWING

If you feel that your carpentry skills are not equal to the task of constructing the arch or A-frame swings shown earlier, do not despair. You can build this swing using simpler techniques from rustic poles – slim tree trunks that have been trimmed and de-barked.

Materials
Hardcore
Concrete

Frame for climbing rope/ladder: from rustic poles 100 mm - 150 mm (4 in - 6 in) in diameter
2 x 2.7 m - 3.4 m (9 ft - 11 ft) uprights
1 x 2 m (6 ft 6 in) crossbar

Frame for swing: from rustic poles 100 mm - 150 mm (4 in - 6 in) in diameter
4 legs
1 crossbar
2 locking bars

Adhesive tape
Nails
Eyebolts
Nuts and washers
Rope/swing chain
Ready-made swing seat

Rope for climbing
Rope ladder

The three-seater swing and the matching climbing rope and ladder shown here are built from rustic poles. The uprights are securely set in concrete for strength, and the only joints involved are rounded notches that allow the components to interlock positively and give the structures extra rigidity and security.

Climbing rope and ladder

The structure here is just a variation on the arch swing (page 18), with two uprights and a strong crossbar from which the rope and ladder are suspended. As the detail to the main photograph shows, the uprights and posts are notched to about one-third of their thickness, and the components are held together with two strong bolts passing through each joint. The rope and ladder are wrapped around the crossbar several times and secured by nails. Nothing could be simpler!

A three-seater swing

The three-seater swing has angled legs at each end, with the same notched and bolted joint at the point where the two components overlap. The crossbar is simply set in the vee-joint formed by the overlapping legs, and as well as being nailed in place it is also secured by two short horizontal locking bars nailed to the tops of the legs.

Here the swing chains are attached to the crossbar with traditional eyebolts and shackles. The swing is fitted with two standard plank seats plus a chair seat for a toddler. The design can be varied to provide just one or two seats instead if you prefer; all you need are uprights spaced closer together and a shorter crossbar.

Building the rope and ladder arch

Start by deciding what features you want

Above: *This sturdy, rustic arch with rope ladder and swing attached will stand up to heavy use by older children and keep-fit enthusiasts.*

Right: *All the joints are formed by notching the components and then bolting through them.*

to incorporate within the design – a good case for consulting the customer, who may want an extra rope or ladder. This will enable you to work out the ideal dimensions for the structure; you need to allow roughly 1 m (just over 3 ft) of crossbar for each hanging element. As for the height of the crossbar, you can tailor this to the ages and sizes of the children who will be playing on it. So long as a soft landing area is laid beneath the frame, you can safely make it between 1.8 m and 2.4 m (6 ft to 8 ft) high for all but the smallest children. Remember to allow for about 900 mm (3 ft) of post to be buried in the ground.

1 Lay out the components on the ground and mark the joint positions on the trunks with adhesive tape, allowing an overlap of about 300 mm (12 in) at each corner.

2 Make a semi-circular mark on the curve of each log, saw down to the mark and

Below: A three-seater swing, one of which is a chair seat, is ideal for a family with children of different ages. The angled construction makes for additonal safety.

Right: The swing crossbar rests in the angle between the legs and is secured with short locking pieces nailed into place.

chisel out the waste; the joint does not have to be an accurate fit.

3 Lay the cut joints together, check that they are at right angles, drill two bolt holes through each joint and assemble them.

4 Dig two holes at the required spacings and set the posts in concrete, bracing them upright until it has set.

5 Finally, attach the hanging ropes and ladders, wrapping each rope round the crossbar several times and securing it with nails.

Building the swing
These instructions apply whether you decide to have one, two or three seats; simply adjust the size of the arch, as described earlier.

6 Mark the joints as for the arch, but with the legs meeting at an angle of 60°, cut them and bolt each pair of legs together.

7 Set each arch in position in concrete, brace it upright and leave to set.

8 After about 48 hours, cut the crossbar carefully to length, lay it in place, and secure it with nails. Finally, add the short locking pieces.

9 Finish off the structure by hanging the swing seats from eyebolts fitted to holes in the crossbar.

SEE-SAWS

Try your hand at a toddler's see-saw which requires basic skills and only a few simple materials. This see-saw works on a central pivot and the seat can be removed quite easily should you want to store it away.

Materials
Hardcore
Concrete

From planed softwood
1 x 2.4 m x 225 mm x 50 mm (8 ft x 9 in x 2 in) seat
2 x 2.4 m x 100 mm x 50 mm (8 ft x 4 in x 2 in) supporting beams
2 x 900 mm x 225 mm x 50 mm (3 ft x 9 in x 2 in) uprights
2 x semi-circles of wood for handholds

Scrap piece of board
12 mm (½ in) diameter steel rod for pivot
6 mm (¼ in) diameter steel rod for locking pins
Screws
Nails
Woodworking adhesive

As mentioned earlier, it is difficult to make do-it-yourself versions of the traditional playground see-saw, since these are often fairly massive constructions with spring-loaded mechanisms designed for use by several children at a time. A full-sized home-made see-saw without some form of spring-loading would be unwieldy and potentially dangerous, and so it is best to restrict your ambitions to making a simple, small-scale see-saw suitable for toddlers which relies on nothing more complicated than a central pivot for its action.

Below: *This simple see-saw for toddlers has smooth, well-rounded edges and is set securely in concrete.*

Making a toddler's see-saw
A see-saw, even one designed for use by small children, needs to be sturdy enough to withstand all sorts of rough treatment.

The design shown here has a long plank for the seat. Any whipping that might occur in such a long beam is prevented by the use of two supporting timbers which

1

give extra reinforcement along its length.

Simple hand-holds at each end of the beam give the riders something to hold on to; these can be semi-circles of wood, loops of rope or something similar improvised from your store of odds and ends; all that matters is that they provide a good grip and prevent a fall when the see-saw is in use.

1 Glue and screw the supporting beams to the underside of the seat, aligning the longer outer edges (photo 2).

2 Drill two holes in the supporting beams to take the wide steel rod and two holes to take the narrow rod (see diagram).

3 Before sinking the uprights into the ground, you must cut out two round-bottomed notches at the top of each upright to take the steel rod (see diagram).

4 Take the two uprights and set them in concrete a fraction over 225 mm (9 in) apart. Each upright is buried to roughly half its length in the ground. To help keep the uprights accurately separated while they are being positioned, fasten a piece of board across their bottom ends and set the complete assembly in a hole about 300 mm (12 in) square.

5 Pack the concrete in the hole, checking that the uprights are vertical, and leave the concrete to harden for at least 48 hours.

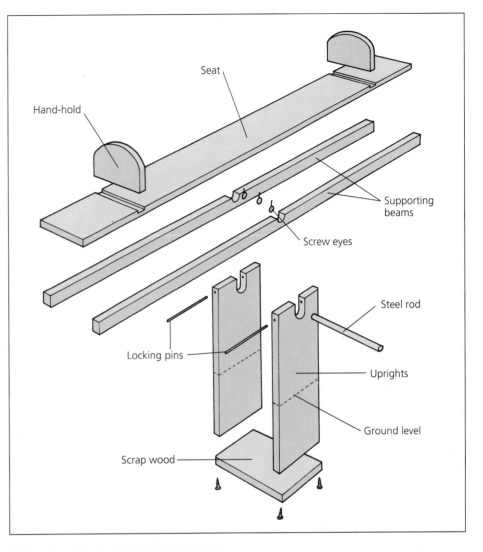

Seat

Hand-hold

Supporting beams

Screw eyes

Steel rod

Locking pins

Uprights

Ground level

Scrap wood

2

6 The pivoting action is provided by the wider diameter steel rod which rests in the two round-bottomed notches cut in the tops of the uprights (photo 1). It passes through the holes in the reinforcing beams and is additionally secured to the underside of the seat by being passed through three carefully aligned screw eyes.

7 Prevent the rod from jumping out of the notches in the uprights by passing two lengths of the narrow steel rod through the holes in the edges of the uprights. These can be withdrawn easily with the aid of a punch to allow the see-saw seat to be removed for storage.

8 Make sure that all the surfaces of the see-saw are smooth and that all edges are rounded off to prevent splinters.

9 Treat the uprights with a preservative to guard against rot and insect attack (see page 10), and paint the seat in a bright primary color. You can add decals or painted designs if you wish to make the see-saw even more attractive to its users.

SLIDE

A play slide for younger children is easily put together using only the simplest materials and basic woodworking techniques. The one shown here is designed so that the two parts – the steps and slide – can be assembled and dismantled quickly for easy storage.

Materials
Frame: from planed softwood
2 x 1.2 m x 76 mm x 25 mm (4 ft x 3 in x 1 in) legs
2 x 750 mm x 76 mm x 25 mm (2 ft 6 in x 3 in x 1 in) legs
2 x 76 mm x 25 mm (3 in x 1 in) cross braces

Steps:
Series of 560 mm (22 in) round softwood rungs
Plywood for backing steps
Woodworking adhesive
Panel pins

Slide:
1 x 1.8 m x 510 mm x 20 mm (6 ft x 20 in x ¾ in) exterior-quality plywood
2 x 1.8 m x 76 mm x 25 mm (6 ft x 3 in x 1 in) planed softwood for sides
Plastic laminate
Contact adhesive
Screws

Wooden hook:
510 mm x 125 mm x 25 mm (20 in x 5 in x 1 in) softwood

Full-size slides, like see-saws, are difficult to copy on a domestic scale. For a start, the size of the structure would dominate the average yard. The support framework for a reasonable-sized slide would need to be relatively massive and therefore prohibitively expensive, and the amateur builder would have difficulty constructing and mounting the slide channel itself, which in public versions is usually of galvanized metal, molded plastic or stainless steel. The only situation where you could contemplate installing a slide of some sort in your yard is down a bank, if your yard has such a feature.

Unless you are a competent metalworker, you would be well advised to contact local firms fabricating sheet metal, with a view to commissioning them to make up a

Above: *Relatively simple to construct, this slide designed with toddlers in mind can be easily moved around the yard. It is also small enough to be used indoors.*

1

slide channel to match the available slope. It would then be a relatively straightforward job to set it in place in a shallow trench excavated in the face of the bank, and to secure it with ground anchor pegs.

You can, however, easily make up a play slide suitable for small children.

Making a toddler's slide
This simple slide consists of two main components, the steps and the slide itself. The overall size of the structure is obviously a matter of personal choice, but as a rough guide for typical toddlers, make the longer arm of the A-frame about 1.2 m (4 ft) long and the shorter one about 750 mm (2 ft 6 in) long.

The steps are an A-shaped frame. One side of each A is extended and rounded off at its top end to form simple hand grips, allowing the children to climb safely on to

4 After fastening the brace in place, saw its ends off flush with the sides of the A-frame, as shown in the diagrams.

5 When you have completed the two A-frames, glue the rungs into place to link the two frames, using waterproof wood-working adhesive.

6 Take direct measurements from the assembled frame and cut an offcut of exterior-quality plywood to size to match the dimensions of the other side of the steps. Tack and glue it into place.

2

Slide
Make the slide to match exactly the separation between the step uprights, which should be 510 mm (20 in) if you have followed the dimensions given earlier.

7 Prepare the two 1.8 m (6 ft) lengths of planed softwood, round off one end of each length as shown in the diagrams and attach them at each side of the slide by driving screws up into them through the plywood. Make sure that these two components are sanded perfectly smooth, and round off their top edges slightly (diagram).

8 To make the slide slippery, cut a piece of plastic laminate to match the size of the slide surface and glue it to the plywood with contact adhesive. Polish it with a little wax polish to keep it friction-free.

9 Complete the slide by adding a wooden 'hook' to its top end. Glue and screw it to the ends of the side rails, and simply hook it over the topmost rung of the steps section to make the slide operational.

10 Finish preservative (see page 10), or paint the slide bright primary colors. For extra versatility, paint the plywood panel linking the two A-frames with blackboard paint so it can be used as a chalk board.

the slide surface, and the two frames are linked by round softwood rungs on one side and a piece of plywood (for additional reinforcement) on the other.

Frame and steps

1 Drill the holes for the rungs at approximately 150 mm (6 in) centers in the longer arms of the A-frame (photo 1); as each rung is 560 mm (22 in) long overall, the spacing between the A-frames when the steps are assembled will be 510 mm (2 ft).

2 Connect the angled legs of each A-frame with a lap joint, so they meet at approximately 60° (photo 2).

3 Glue and screw a cross-brace to each frame about 150 mm (6 in) above ground level to complete the structure of the frame and guarantee total rigidity.

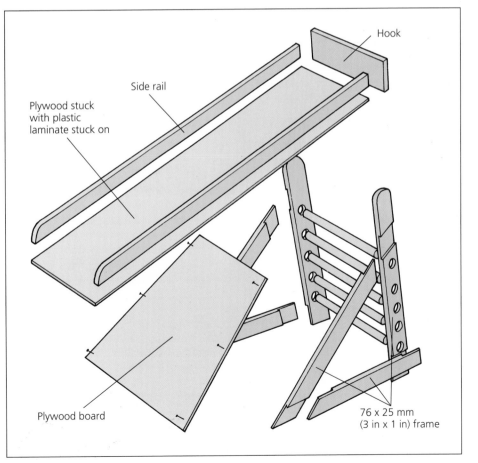

Hook

Side rail

Plywood stuck with plastic laminate stuck on

Plywood board

76 x 25 mm (3 in x 1 in) frame

CLIMBING FRAMES

Few children can resist the challenge of a climb, whatever the obstacle. Many are completely fearless, and will scale – and get down from – astonishing heights with ease. Others find the going up easier than the climbing down, and occasionally have to be rescued. Both groups learn rapidly from their experiences, and soon come to terms with their own abilities as well as the inherent dangers of climbing. Their favorite natural challenges are of course trees, and if your yard lacks any that are suitable for would-be Tarzans, the best alternative is to provide some man-made climbing frames for them.

individual components must be strong enough to support not only a child's weight but also the weight of the frame of which it is a part. Joints must be rigid, so that they cannot skew under load, and careful bracing may need to be added to keep the structure square.

Individual frame components must also be small enough to be gripped by children's hands. Wood with a round cross-section generally offers a better hand-hold than square and rectangular shapes, and has the additional benefit of not having edges that can splinter readily. It is also easier to secure round rungs into uprights and horizontal beams, since a drilled hole is simpler to make than a mortise.

When designing a climbing frame, make it to a scale that suits the ages and physical sizes of the children who will be playing on it. This means spacing rungs, bars and other frame components so they can be reached easily; as a rough guide, aim for a rung spacing of about one third of the average child's height, so that over-stretching does not lead to falls.

Make sure that all fastenings you use are secure; screws and bolts are preferable to nails, which can pull out under a load. Recess the heads of all fastenings if possible to guard against the risk of accidental injury; countersink screw heads and recess bolt heads and nuts in deep counterbores. This also makes them fairly resistant to the attentions of the mischievous adventurer with a wrench. If you use bolts, fit locking washers under nuts to prevent them from

Climbing frames can be as simple or as complex as you wish; what you build depends on your woodworking skills and to a lesser extent on your children's expectations. Many will be happy with the simplest structure, while others will want something more daunting.

Whatever you decide to construct, safety is as always paramount. The structure itself must either be stable enough not to topple over under even the most extreme loading, or must be securely fixed to the ground. Children are notorious for testing things almost to destruction, so you must design to Titanic standards and then more! It is without a doubt best to build permanent structures with posts anchored

Above: *More of an obstacle course, this climbing net will challenge older children.*

Right: *A wonderful fantasy tower, which will spark ideas for imaginative play.*

in the ground, but if you need to be able to dismantle and store a free-standing frame between play periods, try to follow the simple rule of making it at least as wide across the base as it is high, to ensure a relatively low centre of gravity even when the topmost part of the structure is fully loaded with bodies.

The actual structure needs some careful planning too. It goes without saying that

working loose. And finally, treat all metal fastenings with rust-inhibiting paint.

Whether the structure you build is permanent or intended to be dismantled and stored away when it is not in use, check its condition regularly to make sure that all joints are secure and that there is no evidence of rot or insect attack anywhere in the structure. Treat it with a fresh coat of wood preservative (see page 10) every year to ensure that it remains sound and in good condition.

Extra features
While most traditional climbing frames provide a continuous lattice structure, you need not be restricted to this. Apart from climbing things, children love to hang from them. Horizontal ladders high enough for dangling legs to clear the ground are a popular feature, as are knotted ropes and hanging rings, and it is relatively easy to incorporate free space within a typical climbing frame for such features.

Another favorite outdoor challenge is a climbing net – a coarse rope mesh stretched between two simple frames so that climbers can clamber up one side, over the top and down the other in true commando style. The net can either be fixed vertically, or can be used to clad both sides of a steep A-frame structure – a better bet if several children are likely to use the net at the same time, since both sides can be climbed without too much clashing of hands and feet. Nets have another advantage over wooden climbing frames in that they are surprisingly safe to

Above: *This climbing frame for 6-8 year-olds has been cleverly sited at the bottom of the yard, so giving the children some privacy while still being in view of the house.*

use; if a child slips or misses a hand-hold, another is never far away.

Alternative materials
Discarded car tires can also be a useful material for making some unusual climbing apparatus, as is shown on pages 38-39. They are easy to fasten to supporting frameworks and present no hard edges, but it is vital that they are thoroughly steam-cleaned before use, or you will always be cleaning horrible stains from your children's skin and clothes!

LATTICE CLIMBING FRAME

The best way of building a traditional lattice-style climbing frame is on a modular basis. The 'cube' structure shown here is made up from four two-dimensional frames which are then linked together to form a three-dimensional assembly. It all looks more complicated than it really is!

Materials
Cutting list – Frame A
4 x 1.8 m x 50 mm x 50 mm (6 ft x 2 in x 2 in) uprights
2 x 1.8 m x 76 m x 25 mm (6 ft x 3 in x 1 in) rails
3 x 1.768 m (5 ft 10 in) rungs, 32 mm (1¼ in) in diameter

Cutting list – Frames B & C (identical)
2 x 1.8 m x 50 mm x 50 mm (6 ft x 2 in x 2 in) outer uprights
2 x 2.25 m x 50 mm x 50 mm (7 ft 5 in x 2 in x 2 in) inner uprights
4 x 1.768 m (5 ft 10 in) rungs, 32 mm (1¼ in) in diameter
1 x 649 mm x 76 mm x 25 mm (25½ in x 3 in x 1 in) top board

Cutting list – Frame D
4 x 1.8 m x 50 mm x 50 mm (6 ft x 2 in x 2 in) uprights
2 x 1.8 m x 76 m x 25 mm (6 ft x 3 in x 1 in) rails
3 x 1.22 m (4 ft) rungs, 32 mm (1¼ in) in diameter

Linking components
2 x 695 mm x 76 mm x 25 mm (27 in x 3 in x 1 in) top boards
2 x 1.995 m x 76 mm x 25 mm (6ft 6 in x 3 in x 1 in) outer top rails
2 x 1.995 m x 76 mm x 25 mm (6 ft 6 in x 3 in x 1 in) inner top rails
2 x 1.995 m x 76 mm x 25 mm (6 ft 6 in x 3 in x 1 in) outer bottom rails
2 x 1.995 m x 76 mm x 25 mm (6 ft 6 in x 3 in x 1 in) inner bottom rails
12 x 1.22 m (4 ft) through dowels, 32 mm (1¼ in) in diameter

Slot-in platform:
2 x 710 mm x 76 mm x 25 mm (28 in x 3 in x 1 in) for sides
10 x 580 mm x 50 mm x 25 mm (22½ in x 2 in x 1 in) slats

Rope ladder:
Rope
Series of 400 mm x 50 mm x 25 mm (16 in x 2 in x 1 in) softwood ladder rungs

Screws
Woodworking adhesive

Start by taking a close look at the basic structure, as shown in the main diagram. You will see that the first frame – A in the diagram – has four main uprights each 1.8 m (just under 6 ft) tall. These are linked at the top and bottom by horizontal rails and have three equally-spaced, continuous horizontal rungs running through them.

The two frames – B and C – that form the heart of the cube are similar in construction, but the two inner uprights on each frame are extended in height to 2.25 m (just under 7 ft 6 in) to form a central 'tower' in the middle of the assembled structure. The uprights are linked by four sets of continuous rungs as shown; there are no top or bottom rails as on frame A, since these two frames will be adequately braced to frames A and D by additional rungs and braces that will be fastened later as the final structure is assembled.

The fourth frame – D – is similar to frame A in construction, with the exception that the rungs span only three of the four uprights to allow easy access to what will be an open hanging space.

Once the four main frames have been assembled individually, they are connected together both by top and bottom link rails and also by continuous cross-rungs threaded through holes drilled in their uprights. All the ground-level link rails are screwed to the frame uprights. The outer top link rails are also screwed to the faces of the uprights. The inner ones are screwed only to the uprights of frames A and D, and are notched to fit over the rungs of frames B and C. Note that the cross-rungs link only frames A, B and C, so leaving the space between frames C and D open.

Left: *A traditional, modular-style wooden climbing frame; it can be moved around the yard to avoid undue wear and tear on one area of the lawn.*

Assembling the main frame

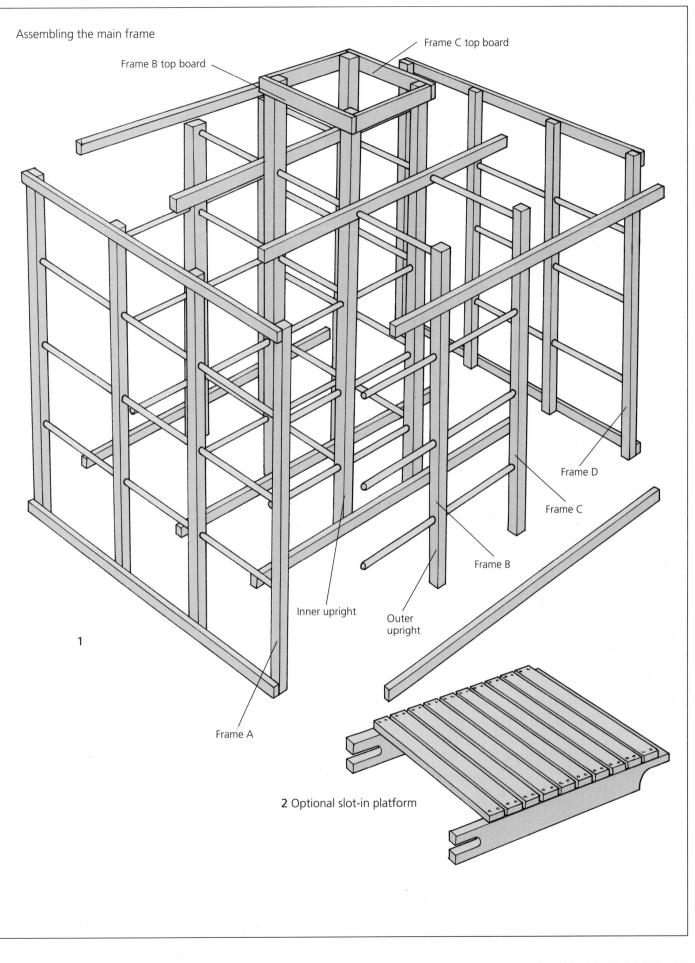

Frame B top board

Frame C top board

Frame D

Frame C

Frame B

Inner upright

Outer upright

Frame A

1

2 Optional slot-in platform

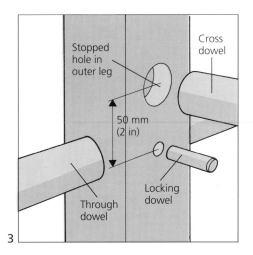

Stopped
hole in
outer leg

Cross
dowel

50 mm
(2 in)

Through
dowel

Locking
dowel

3

The final part of the assembly involves adding top boards round the outside of the four uprights in the center of the structure. You can then add your own personal finishing touches, such as a rope ladder, a hanging tire or a slot-in floor platform which can be fastened anywhere within the lattice structure. You will find details of these on pages 34-35.

Making the individual frames
Because of the large number of components involved in making this climbing frame, precise labelling of the parts is essential to avoid confusion. The best solution is to cut the components and make up each individual frame in turn, and only then prepare the components that link them together. The cutting lists on page 32 give details of the components for each frame in turn, and then for the link components needed to connect them all together. Use only metric measurements for complete accuracy; imperial measurements are given only as an *approximate* conversion.

Assembly sequence
1 Cut the components to length for frame A first, and mark the positions of the rungs on each upright. Rung 1 should be 410 mm (16 in) from the bottom, rung 2 450 mm (17½ in) above rung 1 and rung 3 450 mm (17½ in) above rung 2.

2 Drill the holes for the rungs, using a drill stand (diagram 3). The 32 mm (1¼ in) diameter holes in which they fit are stopped in the two outer uprights, so fit a depth stop to your drill. The holes pass right through the two inner uprights.

3 Thread the rungs through the inner uprights and glue their ends into the stopped holes in the outer uprights.

4 Space out the two inner uprights evenly – they should be 539 mm (21¼ in) apart –

and glue and screw the top and bottom rails to all the uprights to complete frame A.

5 Make up frames B, C and D in a similar way. Note that the uprights of frames B and C are linked by four rungs and also by a top board; there are no full-width rails as on frame A. Frame D is similar to frame A, but the rungs span only three of the four uprights, so two uprights need stopped holes and only one has through holes.

6 Prepare frames A, B and C to receive the through dowels that will link them together in the completed structure. To ensure that these rungs clear those in the individual frames, they are set about 50 mm (2 in) lower down.

Mark the hole positions on each frame as follows, measuring from the bottom of the frames upwards; rung 1 360 mm (14 in) from the bottom, rung 2 450 mm (17½ in) above rung 1, and rung 3 450 mm (17½ in) above rung 2.

Drill 30 mm (1⅛ in) deep stopped holes at the marked rung positions on the inner face of frames A and C, and drill through holes in frame B.

7 Cut to length the eight linking rails that will connect the four frames together and give the completed structure rigidity.

8 Connect frames A, B and C together by threading the rungs through the holes in frame B and gluing them into the stopped holes in frames A and C. You will need some help at this stage, to hold the frames upright and set them the correct distance – 532 mm (21 in) – apart from each other.

9 Attach the four top and bottom outer rails to the structure by gluing and screwing them to the outer uprights of frames A, B and C (diagram 4). Then add the two bottom rails that link the inner uprights of the three frames at ground level.

10 Link the tops of the tall inner uprights on frames B and C with the two 677 mm (26½ in) long top boards.

11 Position frame D in line with the projecting ends of the rails you used in step 9 to connect frames A, B and C together. Glue and screw the ends of the rails to the frame D uprights.

12 Place the two remaining inner linking rails across the assembled structure and mark where they will have to be notched to fit over the topmost rugs of frames B and C. Cut the notches, lay the rails in place and screw them to the uprights of frames A and D to complete the assembly.

Making a slot-in platform
You can increase the versatility and play value of this climbing frame by making one or more slot-in floor platforms. These are designed to be slotted into place over the rungs (diagram 2).

13 To make a slot-in platform, drill 32 mm (1¼ in) diameter holes in each of the side timbers, centered 59 mm (2¼ in) in from the ends. Then make saw cuts to turn one hole into a notch, the other into a cut-out, as shown in the diagram on page 33.

14 Next, glue and screw the slats to the platform sides. Space them evenly, leaving gaps between them for drainage.

Adding a rope ladder
Finish the frame off by adding a rope ladder at one end of the open hanging space between frames C and D. Drill holes in the top rail, thread the rope through, wrap it round the rail twice and knot if off securely. Then drill 12 mm (½ in) diameter holes in the rungs 25 mm (1 in) in from each end and thread the rope through. Tie knots to support the rungs at about 300 mm (1 ft) spacings (diagram 5).

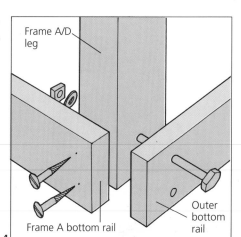

Frame A/D leg

Frame A bottom rail

Outer bottom rail

4

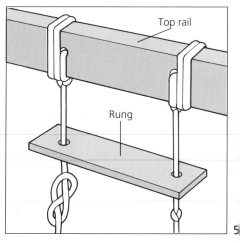

Top rail

Rung

5

A FRAME AROUND A TREE

This climbing frame is on much smaller scale than the lattice frame featured on pages 32-35, and is ideal for younger children. However, that is no guarantee that their older brothers and sisters will not find it irresistible too!

Materials

Frame: from planed softwood
3 x 2.13 m x 76 mm x 76 mm (7 ft x 3 in x 3 in) uprights A
1 x 1.12 m x 76 mm x 76 mm (3 ft 8 in x 3 in x 3 in) upright B
3 x 76 mm x 76 mm (3 in x 3 in) top cross braces H

From two 2440 mm x 1220 mm (8 ft x 4 ft) sheets of MDO (medium density fiberboard) or exterior-quality plywood, cut to match tree
1 x brace C
1 x brace D
2 x lower braces E and F
2 x wide braces G

Roof: from MDF or exterior-quality plywood
1 x roof panel square I to fit
2 x platform panels J and K to fit
1 x end panel N to fit

From sawed softwood
2 x 76 mm x 76 mm (3 in x 3 in) ledgers L and M

Steps:
4 x 400 mm (16 in) wide MDO/plywood for step cut-outs O
4 x 76 mm x 25 mm (3 in x 1 in) wood for vertical step supports P

Further platform boards Q and R to span top deck
Further horizontal braces S and T if constructing on soft ground

Woodworking adhesive
Screws
Nails
Rope, etc. for playthings

Right: This climbing frame doubles as a tree house and also gives access to the tree for older children. It may be possible to add a further platform at a higher level.

The climbing frame shown here is built around a tree, and in this situation it can do double duty both as a climbing frame and as a tree house. Depending on the shape of the tree, you could easily extend the central platform upwards to provide another storey; because the frame is built around the trunk of the tree it is perfectly stable, yet it is not actually fixed to it so you need have no fears of damaging the tree itself.

However, a tree is not essential at all; the structure can equally well be free-standing, set on a lawn or on an area of chipped bark or gravel to guarantee a soft landing to anyone taking an unexpected tumble from the frame.

The frame is constructed from off-the-peg planed softwood, plus some exterior-quality plywood or MDO (medium-density fiberboard) which is used for the side braces, platforms and cut-out steps featured in the design. The sizes given are for guidance only; you can modify them as you wish, either to change the overall shape of the frame or to tailor-make it to fit around a particular tree.

The frame consists of two identical main assemblies which are linked with horizontal braces to form the basic structure. These act as steps to allow the players access to the lower levels at each end of the frame. Cut-out steps then lead up to the higher central section, where platform boards are added to fit around the tree or to provide a top floor if the structure is designed to be free-standing.

Assembly sequence

1 Start by cutting the components of each main assembly. Space uprights A and upright B as shown in photo 1 and link them together by a long brace C, roughly 200 mm (8 in) wide, fastened with its top edge about 800 mm (2 ft 7 in) above ground level, by a similar brace D linking the two inner uprights near their tops, and by two shorter low-level braces E and F fastened with their top edges 400 mm (16 in) from the ground. These lower braces act as steps to provide access to the platforms at each end of the frame. Glue and screw all the components together to complete the two assemblies (photo 2).

2 Next, prop up the two assemblies – at each side of the trunk if you are erecting it around a tree, in the open otherwise – and link them together first of all with the two cross braces G, screwed to the tall center uprights immediately above the long braces C (photo 3). Then add parallel top cross braces H between the tall uprights, fastening them in place with their top edges level with the top edges of the plywood braces D fastened in step 1 (photo 4).

3 Next, make up the two low-level end platforms and the roof above the wider platform. The roof panel is cut and fastened on top of the two top braces H. The two platforms J and K are pieces of board resting on the ledgers L and M that are screwed to the main frame uprights; note that you need to notch the plywood cross braces G next to the inner uprights to allow the inner ends of the platform ledgers to be screwed to these uprights.

3

After attaching all the ledgers, cut the platform panels to size and screw them in place (photo 5). Finish this stage by adding end panel N to the end of the frame, in line with the roof panel.

4 Prepare the four cut-out step assemblies O; they need to be long enough to reach between the top edges of the end plat-

1

2

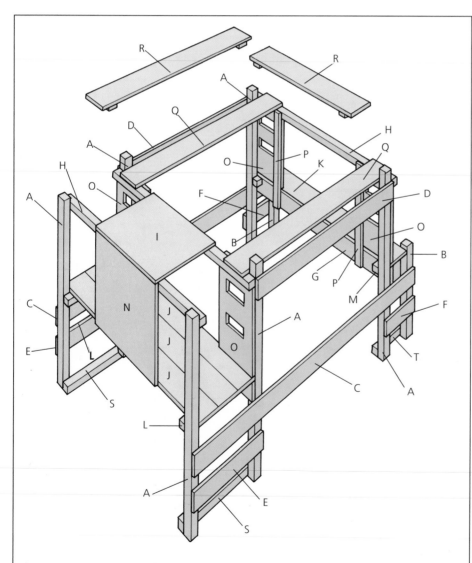

4

5

6

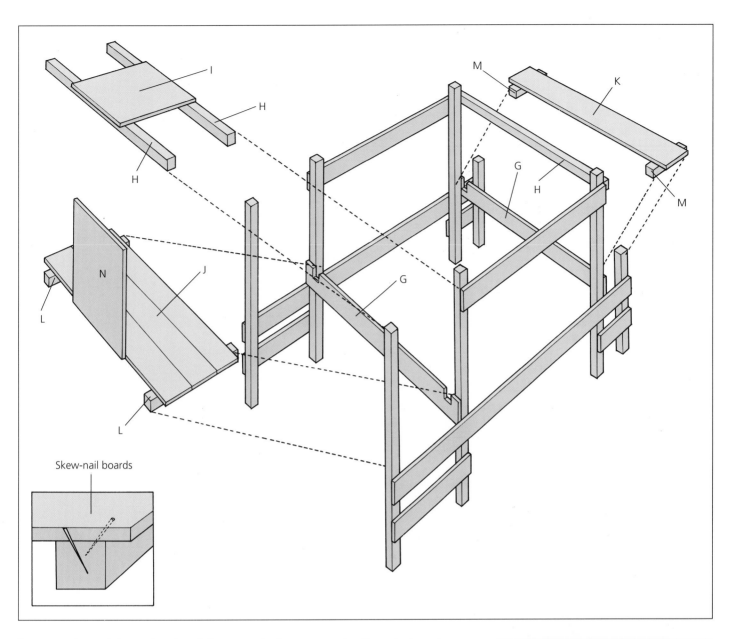

Skew-nail boards

forms J and K and the undersides of the top cross braces H. Make two rectangular cut-outs in each piece of board using a drill and a coping saw or jig saw to form the step rungs. Then screw the four vertical step supports P to the inner faces of the top braces H and the plywood cross braces G, and fasten the steps in place to these and to the inner uprights (photo 6).

This completes the main assembly of the climbing frame.

Further platforms
You can now add further platform boards to the top deck of the frame, fastening them on the top cross braces H (photo 7).

If you are building the frame around a tree trunk, position these to suit the shape of the tree and its main branches, as shown in the photograph. You will see that in this particular situation one plank links the tops of each pair of steps, and a further plank connects the first plank and passes between the tree branches.

If the frame is to be free-standing, you can span the top deck with a series of closely-spaced boards or provide a central cross-bar of 76 x 76 mm (3 in x 3 in) wood, also resting on the top braces H, from which to suspend a rope ladder, a swing or a climbing rope.

If the ground on which the frame is set is particularly soft, you may need to fasten additional horizontal braces to the main uprights to prevent them from sinking into the ground.

You can add any additional features you wish to the frame, such as lengths of rope to aid climbing or additional panels to create enclosed "den" areas. You could even add a simple slide running from the edge of the wider low-level platform down to ground level. Why not just let your imagination run riot?

7

Above: *The top boards are locked in place simply by turning the battens.*

RUSTIC HANGING BARS

If you have neither the time nor the inclination or the skill to construct a fully-fledged climbing frame, your children still need not be disappointed. These rustic hanging bars are so easy to build and will give hours of pleasure.

Materials
Hardcore
Concrete

From 75 mm (3 in) diameter rustic poles
4 x 2.3 m (7 ft 6 in) uprights
2 x 2.4 m (8 ft) horizontals
Smaller poles for angled corner braces
Smaller poles for step up rungs

Hanging bars:
1 m (3 ft) knot-free poles or round
  hardwood mouldings

Fastener bolts
Nuts
Locking washers
Nails

Tire projects:
Old tires
Rustic poles
Hardcore
Concrete
Heavy-duty coach screws

Armed with a supply of trimmed rustic poles and the ability to cut some extremely rudimentary lap joints, you can quickly assemble this simple yet sturdy set of hanging bars.

The main framework consists of four uprights and two horizontals, which for strength's sake should be at least 75 mm (3 in) in diameter. If the horizontals are to span a length of more than about 3 m (10 ft), go up a size to poles about 100 mm (4 in) in diameter.

You should start by deciding how big you want the frame to be, especially its height. This will depend to a certain extent on the average size of the children who will be using it; as a rough guide, construct it so that they will have a drop of no more than about 450 mm (18 in) to the ground when they are hanging from the bars with their arms outstretched. An overall length of about 2.4 m (8 ft) and a width of 1 m

(3 ft 3 in or so) is ideal for most children and will not take up too much garden space, but you can always make it longer if you have the room.

With any structure from which children could fall, it is wise to provide a soft

Right: Rustic poles and old tires have been used to make this climbing structure. The bottom tire is partially sunk in the chippings and forms a join with the concrete.

Above and left: *The rungs are nailed into cut-outs in the main horizontals, which are strengthened by angled braces.*

surface underneath, Here the bars are surrounded by a landing area filled with chipped bark.

Making the hanging bars
1 Start by cutting the four uprights to length; remember to allow for about

600 mm (2 ft) of their total length to be buried in the ground. Then cut rounded notches about 150 mm (6 in) down from their top ends to accept the horizontals, and make two smaller notches lower down in one of the posts to which a step-up rung will be fastened later.

2 Next, set the uprights in place in holes about 600 mm (2 ft) deep, pack in some broken brick and rubble and surround them with concrete. Brace each one with lengths of scrap timber so that they stand vertical, and leave the concrete to harden for 48-72 hours.

3 Cut the two main horizontals to length, lay them side by side and mark the positions for the notches into which the hanging bars will fit. Space these at roughly 300 mm (12 in) centers, and cut them out to a rough square shape.

4 Either clamp each horizontal to its posts or get a helper to support it in place while you drill holes through post and horizontal to accept the fastening bolts. Fasten each horizontal in place securely with a bolt, nut and locking washer at each end of frame.

5 Complete the structure by nailing the rungs into their notches, adding the diagonal corner braces and fastening the step-up rung at one end. The braces can be simply nailed in place, but will be stronger and will give extra rigidity to the structure if they are set in simple sawed notches cut into the horizontal and uprights (see the close-up photograph).

Using old tires

Once upon a time, every child's yard seemed to have an old car tire suspended by a length of rope from a tree branch or similar support for use as a makeshift swing. Some no doubt still do, but more sophisticated swings have generally taken their place nowadays. However, the humble cast-off tire can also be used to make some unusual climbing obstacles, in conjunction with some simple supporting timberwork. Because tires are resilient (if hard) and have no sharp edges, they make remarkably safe pieces of play apparatus.

If you do decide to use old tires, make sure that they are thoroughly steam-cleaned first in order to remove all traces of oil, tarmac and other materials that could stain your children's hands and skin. It is also well worth scrubbing the tires thoroughly with strong detergent before using them for play.

The two examples shown here give some idea of what can be achieved with just a little ingenuity.

The first features a simple three-sided pyramid shape formed by sturdy de-barked rustic poles set in a concrete base. The largest tire acts as a mould for the concrete, while the others are simply dropped over the top of the poles and then

Above: *Tires screwed to the pole with a piece of metal to prevent rubber tearing.*

Left: *An alternative configuration for rustic poles and old tires.*

pulled down over them as far as they will go to provide hand- and foot-holds.

The second uses three large tractor tires fastened to the inside of three thick supporting poles. The poles are set in concrete, and the tires are secured to them by driving heavy-duty coach screws through the tire walls into the posts. For strength, and to stop the tire walls from splitting in use, fasten two screws at each fastening point and drive them through a piece of scrap metal as shown in the close-up photograph.

ADVENTURE PLAYGROUND

If you have the space available in your yard, a relatively inexhaustible source of raw materials at a reasonable price, and above all the time to devote to making your children's dreams come true, then this adventure playground is the project you have been waiting for. It offers children of all ages a marvelous range of outdoor play activities within an elaborate multi-purpose structure, and not only are the various components very simple to construct; they can also be rearranged, adapted and extended to suit any site and satisfy the requirements of the most demanding of children.

As you can see from the photographs on this page and the ground plan overleaf, the adventure playground consists of two main structures – the fort and the hut. Each is built off the ground on sturdy stilts, bringing a third dimension to the various games that can be played in, on and under each building. There are sturdy steps leading up to deck level in each one, and a slide that guarantees a quick escape either from the fort at one end of the complex or from the open platform at the other end.

The two buildings are linked by a novel feature – a chain bridge – which will surely be the site of many a heroic battle for supremacy between the hut-dwellers and the custodians of the fort. However, this is not the only route that attackers of either building could take. The fort can be stormed commando-style via an angled climbing net strung from one of its walls, while the platform next to the hut can be scaled by the agile using a rope ladder suspended from a timber arch.

Of course, the playground is not only the perfect site for every game of attack and defense. It can be an obstacle course run in a variety of directions, a camp site, a log cabin in the woods, a pirate ship, or simply a series of endlessly enjoyable individual play activities including climbing, swinging, hanging, jumping and hiding.

Construction basics

Each of the two main structures is built in basically the same way. The main elements of the construction are the sturdy vertical corner support posts. These are trimmed and de-barked tree trunks measuring between 100 and 150 mm (4 to 6 in) in diameter, which are set to a depth of at least 900 m (3 ft) and secured with concrete. The floor decks in the fort and hut, and the open platform beyond the latter, are made up of planed planks resting on rectangular sawed timber ledgers that are bolted to the corner posts. The walls of each building are formed by nailing split rustic poles (and any other timber that comes to hand) to horizontal rails fastened between the posts, while the hut roof is covered with fencing boards nailed to a simple supporting framework.

Throughout the playground improvisation is the key but safety is the watchword. The entire structure is extremely solid; all the main joints are either bolted or screwed together and all the timbers used are sturdy enough to cope with any imaginable weight they might have to bear. Both the flights of steps have handrails, as does the chain bridge, and all the raised platform areas have walls around them except where jump-off points – next to the rope ladder, for example – require clear access.

The two slides are one-piece plastic mouldings bought from toy or playground equipment suppliers, and the climbing net is of rot-proof polypropylene, securely lashed to its supporting framework. Finally, the entire playground is surrounded by an area of crushed bark to provide a surface that wears well underfoot, drains well in wet weather and provides a soft and safe landing when the inevitable falls occur.

Right: Children of all ages can enjoy this adventure playground – the perfect site for games of attack and defense.

Before you start

As mentioned earlier, you do not have to build this type of outdoor play structure all at once. Its very nature makes it an add-on project; you could start with the fort, build the hut later and add the open platform the following season. Every element is completely adaptable, allowing you to position the steps and slides wherever you like and to add extra features such as hanging rings and swings as the fancy takes you – or as your children insist.

Give some thought to wood preservation. The underground parts of the posts will be particularly vulnerable to rot and insect attack, and the rest of the structure will of course be exposed to the weather

once assembly is complete. For components that will not be handled by children, buy preservative-treated timber if possible. Elsewhere soak the ends of all the in-ground posts in wood preservative for 24 hours before installing them, and give the rest of the structure a generous coat of preservative once assembly is complete. Pay particular attention to treating cut ends and drilled holes where porous end-grain is exposed. See also page 10.

Setting out the site
Materials
Split poles for perimeter edging
In-ground pegs
Crushed bark chippings

To support posts:
Hardcore
Concrete
Scrap timber

1 Start by deciding how much you plan to build as the first phase of the project, and study the main photos and the ground plan (diagram 1) so you can work out roughly what materials will be required.

2 Choose the site for the playground, clear any vegetation and excavate the topsoil down to a depth of about 150 mm (6 in). Edge the excavation with split poles secured to in-ground pegs to provide a clear perimeter (and to retain the bed of

crushed bark chippings which will be laid later on).

3 Next, mark out the site with pegs to indicate where the main supporting posts will go for each element of the structure, and check that everything is roughly aligned and square; total precision does not matter too much so long as the overall impression is satisfactory.

Securing the main posts
Every element of the playground relies for its stability on the strength of the main supporting posts. Once these are correctly set in place, the rest of the construction is quite straightforward.

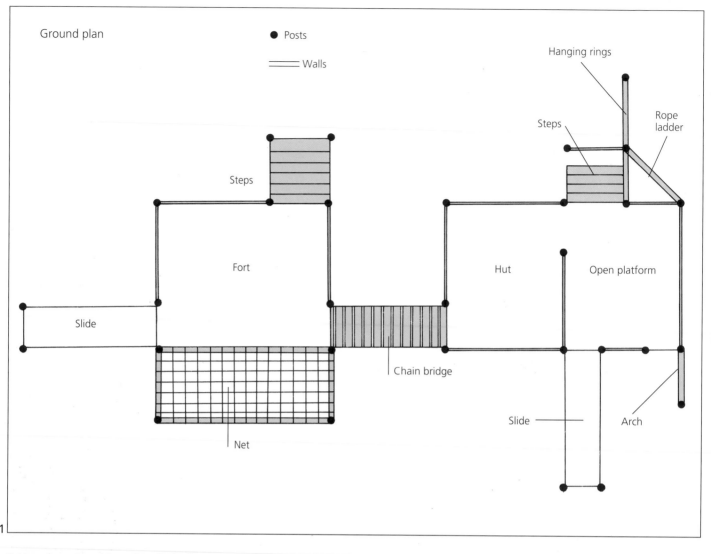

Ground plan
● Posts
═══ Walls

Hanging rings

Steps

Rope ladder

Steps

Fort

Hut

Open platform

Slide

Chain bridge

Slide

Arch

Net

1

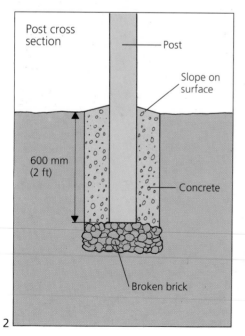

Post cross section

Post

Slope on surface

600 mm (2 ft)

Concrete

Broken brick

2

4 At each post position, dig a hole about 300 mm (12 in) square and about 900 mm (3 ft) deep. Place some broken bricks or similar inert material in the base of the hole to assist with drainage and help to keep the foot of the post dry and free from rot. Then stand the post in place and brace it upright with scrap timber. Shovel in some coarse concrete, tamp it down well and smooth the top off at a slight slope to drain rainwater away from the post (diagram 2).

5 Repeat this process for all the other main posts you need, then leave the concrete to set for 48-72 hours before starting any actual construction work.

Building the fort
Materials
Vertical support posts
Posts at access points
Floor support ledgers
Infill wall and floor timbers
Half-round capping rail
Posts for wall clapboarding
2 x handrail posts
2 x handrails
2 x 76 mm x 25 mm (3 in x 1 in) board to carry step treads
Split logs to form rungs

Slide:
Plastic moulded slide
2 x short posts to support bottom of slide
Angle brackets to fasten slide to deck

Climbing Net:
Netting to fit
2 x thick poles for cross pieces
2 x thick poles for side pieces
2 x short supporting poles

The fort is an open-topped, walled platform with access points on three sides for the steps, the slide and the chain bridge leading to the hut. It has a support post at each corner, plus an extra post next to each access point. Five of the posts project about 2 m (6 ft 6 in) above ground, while the two posts carrying the climbing net are a little taller than the others to give climbers something extra to hold on to.

1 Once you have set the support posts in place, bolt the floor support ledgers in place about 1 m (3 ft 3 in) above ground level. Fix two to the outsides of the main

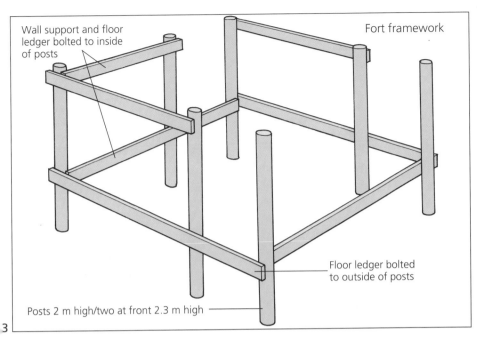

Fort framework

Wall support and floor ledger bolted to inside of posts

Floor ledger bolted to outside of posts

Posts 2 m high/two at front 2.3 m high

3

corner posts and the other two (at right angles to these) to the insides of the posts.

2 Bolt or screw similar ledgers in place between the corner posts and those next to the access points, level with the post tops, to support the walls round the sides of the platform (diagram 3), and nail on the infill timbers.

3 Nail a half-round capping rail on top of the wall timbers, except along the wall where the climbing net will be fastened, and make sure you carefully recess in all the nail heads for safety.

4 To make the flight of steps leading up to the fort deck, set two short handrail posts

Below: *This playground provides plenty of scope for more solitary activities.*

in concrete in line with those at each side of the access point and about 1 m (3 ft 3 in) away from the deck edge.

5 Nail two lengths of 76 mm x 25 mm (3 in x 1 in) wood between the high and low posts to carry the step treads, then nail on split logs to form the rungs. Finish the flight off by fastening a handrail at each side.

6 Next, install the slide. Its bottom end rests on two short posts set in concrete; position them to suit the height and length of the slide. Then fasten the slide securely to the fort deck and the short support posts using screws and angle brackets or the fastenings provided by the slide supplier.

Making the climbing net (diagram 4)
Start by locating a rope supplier. You will generally find one listed in a local telephone directory; try ship/yacht dealers, boatbuilders or marine supply stores other-

Above: *The slide is off to one side and has plenty of space at the end of the chute.*

Left: *Make sure the handrails are strong enough to take the weight of a child.*

wise. Alternatively, you can make up a small square of netting yourself by knotting lengths of rope together, although the results are not likely to be as neat or strong as a bought net.

7 Make up a frame for the net using four lengths of thick pole. You need two cross-pieces the same length as the width of the fort wall, and two side pieces long enough to reach from the top of the fort wall down to the ground at an angle of about 60°.

8 Make a rounded cut-out in the top ends of the two frame sides, and nail the top cross-piece into the cut-outs. Lay the other

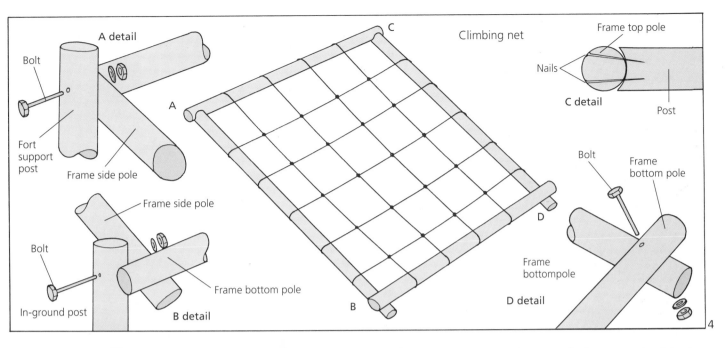

A detail

Bolt
Fort support post
Frame side pole
A

Climbing net

C

Frame top pole
Nails
C detail
Post

Frame side pole
Bolt
In-ground post
Frame bottom pole
B detail
B

D

Bolt
Frame bottom pole
Frame bottompole
D detail

4

cross-piece over the bottom ends of the frame sides and bolt it to them. Then lash the net to the frame with a series of rope loops (see diagram 4).

9 Position the completed net frame against the wall of the fort and fix bolts through the fort corner posts and the frame sides to hold it in place. At the ground end of the net frame, set short supporting posts in concrete and bolt the frame to them.

Building the hut
Materials
4 x vertical corner support posts
2 x intermediate posts for access points
Floor ledgers
Deck planks for floor
Parallel wall ledgers
Wall boards
Long boards for gables
Rafters
Fencing boards for roof

Chain bridge:
2 lengths short chain
Series of 76 mm x 25 mm (3 in x 1 in) planed timber for footholds
2 handrails
Chain shackles with locking pins
Eyebolts

Ladders/Hanging Rings:
Horizontal beam
Galvanized steel straps
Extra vertical support post

Left: The climbing net has been fastened at an angle to make it safer and easier for children to use.

The hut construction is very similar in principle to that of the fort (see diagram 5).

1 There are four main corner posts, plus two intermediate posts next to the two access points in the side walls – see the ground plan again. The planked deck is supported on similar floor ledgers bolted to the posts about 1 m (3 ft 3 in) above ground level, and the corner posts are linked by parallel ledgers higher up to which the wall boards are nailed.

2 Cut longer boards at an angle to form the gable ends of the building, and cut simple rafters to size to support the fencing boards that cover the roof.

3 Cut some of the wall boards short at the top to create rudimentary windows along the rear wall of the hut – these are ideal for spotting marauders sneaking up on the rear access steps!

As it stands, the hut has two open access points in opposite corners. The first is designed to be connected to the fort by the chain bridge, while the latter leads out onto the open platform next to the hut in the completed playground. If you are not ready to build this platform yet, make up a flight of steps leading into the hut in the same way as you did for the fort.

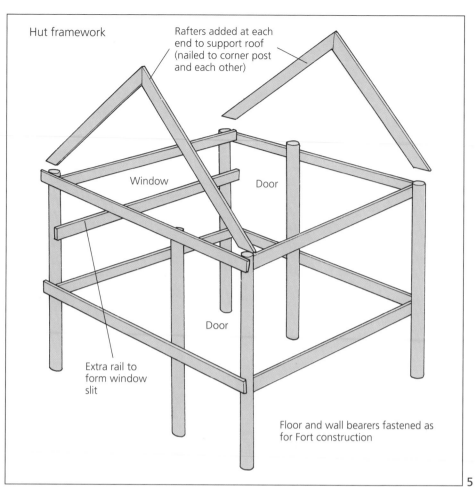

Hut framework

Rafters added at each end to support roof (nailed to corner post and each other)

Window

Door

Door

Extra rail to form window slit

Floor and wall bearers fastened as for Fort construction

5

Above: *The chain bridge makes a wonderful alternative entrance to the building.*

Making the chain bridge

This is an ingenious construction that is far more fun to cross than a fixed bridge. It consists of two lengths of stout chain suspended across the gap between the fort and the hut, to which short planks are secured with nuts and bolts. Two timber handrails are provided at each side of the

bridge for safety; these could equally well be lengths of stout rope fixed between the two structures. Galvanized welded-link chain can be bought from a local chain manufacturer or supplier.

4 Use a hacksaw to cut two pieces of chain long enough to span the gap between the buildings, allowing for a slight droop. Then cut a series of slats from 76 mm x 25 mm (3 in x 1 in) planed timber, and drill a hole about 50 mm (2 in) in from each end of each slat.

5 Attach the slats to the links of the chain

with short bolts and nuts, fastening a locking washer beneath each nut for extra security. Space the slats about 25 mm (1 in) apart, and leave about 50 mm (2 in) of chain free at each end so you can attach the bridge to the buildings (see diagram 6).

6 Fasten two eye bolts into the floor ledgers at each end of the span, and attach the bridge chains to them using chain shackles with screw-in locking pins.

Adding the open platform

You can extend the playground further by adding an open platform to the far side of

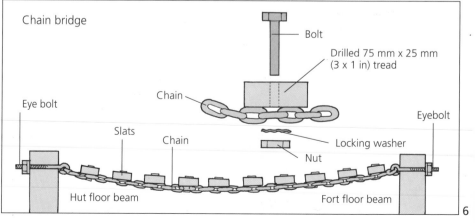

Chain bridge

Bolt

Drilled 75 mm x 25 mm (3 x 1 in) tread

Eye bolt

Chain

Eyebolt

Slats

Chain

Locking washer

Nut

Hut floor beam

Fort floor beam

6

the hut, using exactly the same construction technique as you employed to build the fort. The main support posts are positioned as shown in the ground plan to provide two access points to the front – one for the escape slide, the other as a jumping-off point – and two to the rear, one for a flight of steps and the other to allow climbers access to the platform via a rope ladder (see below).

There is direct access to the hut from the platform, and if you built steps up to the hut door earlier, it is a simple matter to reposition them so they run up to the rear edge of the platform instead, as shown in the photographs and on the ground plan. Here the flight is partly concealed by planked walls – a purely optional feature.

Below: *Access to the open platform is partly concealed by planked walls.*

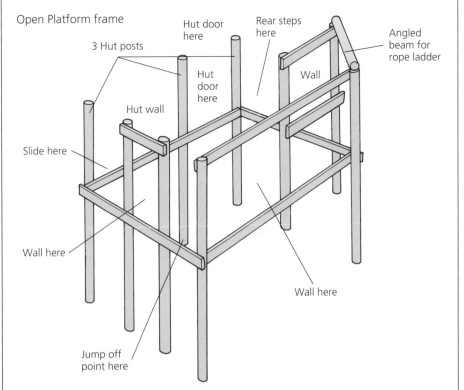

Open Platform frame

3 Hut posts

Hut door here

Rear steps here

Angled beam for rope ladder

Hut door here

Wall

Hut wall

Slide here

Wall here

Wall here

Jump off point here

7

Above: *Secure horizontal beams to the post tops with galvanized metal straps.*

Left: *Make sure that there's plenty of chipped bark for soft landings.*

Ladders and hanging rings

The last features of the playground which you might like to add are a rope ladder at the rear of the open platform, and a pair of hanging rings suspended from a beam next to the rear platform access steps. Both the rope ladder and the rings are suspended from eyebolts set in a horizontal beam that is secured to the tops of vertical posts by simple galvanized steel straps. As you can see from the ground plan, the ladder beam is fixed to the top of two posts forming part of the structure of the open platform, while one extra post is all that is needed to support the beam for the hanging rings.

The safety zone

The entire playground is surrounded with a bed of chipped bark or similar material to provide a safe surface for the children to use. After edging the excavated site with pegged planks, which should be at least 2 m (6 ft 6 in) away from an likely landing areas, simply spread and rake out the chips to a depth of about 150 mm (6 in). Clean up the site by re-raking the chips from time to time, and add to the bed with fresh chips as necessary when bald patches or hollows begin to appear.

PLAYHOUSES

Many children, when asked to choose their favourite piece of outdoor play equipment, will opt for a home or den of their own – a building where they can escape the elements, and the watchful eye of their parents to indulge in their favorite games and fantasies. You can, of course, buy ready-made playhouses, but you will feel a much greater sense of satisfaction – and give your children a building tailor-made to their precise requirements – if you build a playhouse for them yourself.

When you convene the first planning and site meeting with your young customers, their personalities will go a long way towards deciding what they want you to build. Adventurous types with a head for heights are likely to request a tree house. Others may prefer a more down-to-earth approach and will choose a conventional playhouse. This can be anything from a perfectly-built, scaled-down replica of a summerhouse or chalet, to a more ramshackle structure, perhaps built by the children themselves with a little adult help.

Whatever type of building you decide to construct, remember that it must be a safe place for your children to play in. That means paying as much attention to its construction, finishing and security as you would to any other garden project.

Building tree houses

If you have a suitably mature tree in your yard, there is no doubt that a tree house will be enormously popular and building one can be a very interesting project. The secret of success is to tailor-make the house to fit the tree, rather than the other way around; after all, the tree will probably long outlive the house, so you do not want to prune it simply to fit the house in place.

Start by assessing the best place for the house floor, which does not have to be on one level if a split-level design suits the tree shape better. Nail blocks to the branches to form level support and fixing points, and make cut-outs in the floor if necessary to fit it round the branches. Then nail the floor securely in place, and add vertical and horizontal pieces of wood between the tree branches to form a framework for the wall clapboarding. You can use plank or board off-cuts for the walls, or tie on canvas.

Finish the house with a roof, which can be permanent or something more temporary, such as a tarpaulin tied to the tree branches, and add a fixed ladder for access to and from the platform – far safer than a rope ladder, whatever the children may say.

Building at ground level

If your clients request something more traditional and down-to-earth for their playhouse, remember that anything built at ground level should have proper foundations – ideally a concrete slab, although with simple structures you might be able to get away with building 'direct to earth' as long as you can support the structure clear of the ground and so keep dampness at bay.

If you decide to lay concrete, you need a slab about 100 mm (4 in) thick, laid over 75-100 mm (3-4 in) of well-compacted gravel or rubble. Use a 1:2:3 cement:

sand:aggregate mix (or 1:4 cement: combined aggregates), and lay the concrete in formwork so the slab has neat square sides. This will then provide the perfect base for a timber floor on which the rest of the building can be constructed.

For a more temporary structure, you can support the building's floor – tongued-and-grooved boards or exterior-grade plywood nailed to square joists to give it strength and the necessary stiffness – on rows of bricks, garden walling blocks or paving slabs. Tamp these down firmly into the soil, check that they are level with each other and then place a piece of something water-proof – roofing felt or plastic material, for example – on top of each one. Before you lift the floor into position, it is a good idea to lay black polyethylene sheeting over the ground to discourage weeds. Cover the plastic with gravel, place the supports, and

Above: *This tree house is only partially supported by the tree trunks. Shrubs help to disguise the supporting structure.*

Left: *Every little girl's dream playhouse!*

then set the floor in place on top of them.

Construction basics

Probably the best way of building up the structure of a typical playhouse is to follow the principles used by the manufacturers of prefabricated garden buildings, making up the individual wall panels with a simple frame covered in clapboarding, and then adding a flat or pitched roof.

Use preservative-treated wood (see page 10) with a cross-section of at least 50 mm x 25 mm (2 in x 1 in) for the frame, and space the uprights at about 450 mm (18 in) centers between the top and bottom plates to give the wall panel a reasonable degree of rigidity when the clapboarding is added. Exterior-grade plywood is probably the best clapboarding material to use, but you can press anything from old floorboards to fencing timber into service instead.

Within individual wall panels, fit cross-rails to form window and door openings. Use the same framing and clapboarding materials as for the walls to make up a matching door. Fit the windows with unbreakable rigid plastic sheeting, held with beading.

With an extra pair of hands to help you steady the panels, lift the first one on to the edge of the floor. Then place the next panel at right angles to the first and bolt the two together by passing the bolts through holes drilled in the end frame uprights. Repeat the process to fit the other panels, then nail or screw the bottom plate of each panel securely to the floor.

Adding roofs

The simplest type is a flat roof cut from exterior-grade plywood which overhangs the walls all around by about 50 mm (2 in).

If your prefer the look of a pitched roof, you can again use plywood but you really need to provide some support along the ridge line – few children can resist climbing on to a roof sooner or later. To avoid a lot of complex carpentry, make up two gable wall frames by extending the wall structure to an apex with two rafters, and cover it with clapboarding. Then form a home-made joist hanger from three offcuts of wood nailed in a U-shape to the inside of the apex on each gable wall panel, and drop in a ridge board so its top corners are level with the tops of the panels (see diagram). Secure the board by driving a long woodscrew through each side wall into the ends of the board. Then position the roof panels and nail the top edge of each one to the ridge board, the other edges to the tops of the wall panels. Finish with roofing felt.

A SCANDINAVIAN CHALET

This unusual playhouse features the steeply-pitched roof style popular in countries with regular winter snowfalls, and its design has the added advantage of providing excellent headroom inside the building. It would look attractive in any yard setting.

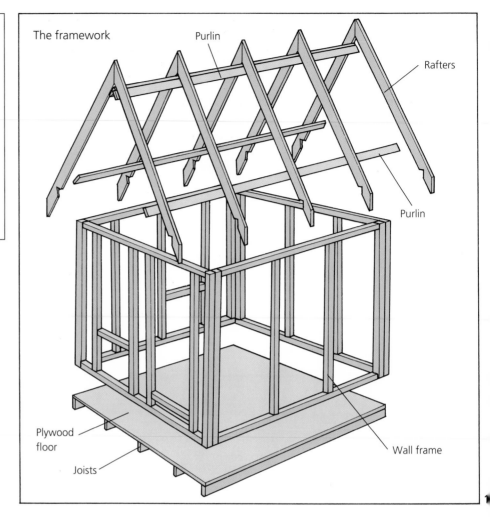

The framework

Purlin

Rafters

Purlin

Plywood floor

Joists

Wall frame

Materials

Concrete base:
Hardcore
Cement
Sand
Aggregate
Scrap timber to create framework

Floor:
12 mm (½ in) thick exterior-quality plywood to fit
50 mm x 50 mm (2 in x 2 in) joists
Dampproofing

Walls:
4 x wall frames made from 50 mm x 50 mm (2 in x 2 in) timber
Small pieces of timber to frame door/window openings
Clapboarding from planks or 6 mm or 9 mm (¼ in or ⅜ in) plywood

Door:
Panel
Clapboarding
Beading

Windows:
Beading
Rigid clear plastic

Roof:
Rafters and purlins from 76 mm x 38 mm (3 in x 1½ in) sawn softwood
Plywood roof panels and bargeboards
Clapboarding (as for walls)
Roofing felt or shingles

Bolts
Nails
Studs
Screws
Panel tacks

The construction follows the basic principles outlined on page 49, using four prefabricated wall panels bolted together at the corners and set on a timber floor. Cross-braces in the front and side wall frames provide door and window openings, and the windows are fitted with rigid PVC sheeting (for safety) to ensure that the building is fully weatherproof.

The roof structure is, because of its steep pitch, rather more complex than the simple panel-and-ridge-board construction

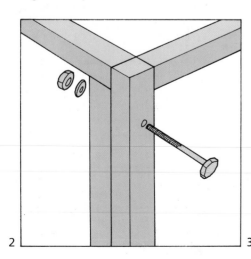

2

3

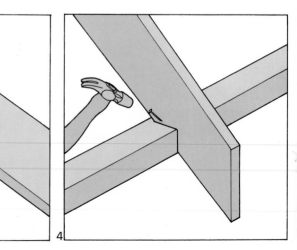

4

described earlier. Here pairs of rafters rest on the tops of the wall panels and are linked by horizontal purlins to form a traditional roof with projecting gables and overhanging eaves (diagram 1). The rafters are then covered with exterior-grade plywood and finished with roofing felt or, if the budget can accommodate the additional expense, cedar shingles.

Building the chalet

The building needs to be set on a concrete base unless it is being erected on an existing paved or concreted area such as a patio.

Assembly sequence

1 After deciding on the overall size of the building, begin by making the floor. Nail the plywood to the floor joists spaced at about 300 mm (12 in) intervals. Set the floor in place on its base, with strips of dampproofing material laid between the joists and the concrete to keep damp and rot at bay.

2 Make up the front and back wall panels to match the width of the floor. To allow for the frames to be bolted together at the corners, the two side wall frames should measure 100 mm (4 in) less from front to back than the length of the floor sides on which they will rest. Match the panel height to the sizes of the occupants; a height of around 1.2 m (4 ft) is a fair compromise.

Nail all the joints together securely, and fit intermediate studs at about 450 mm (18 in) spacings except where you want door or window openings. Add short horizontal pieces to frame these. Then cut the clapboarding to fit each wall panel and tack it on to the framework.

3 With a helper to keep the panels steady, set the front and side panels in place on the floor edges and butt them together.

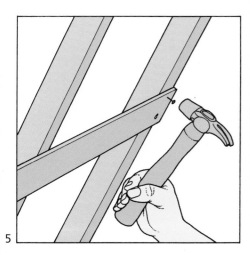

Drill three holes through the two frame corner posts at the top, middle and bottom of the corner and bolt the panels together (diagram 2). Repeat this for the other three corners, then nail or screw down through the bottom of each wall panel into the floor.

4 To form the roof structure, cut pairs of rafters to length. To achieve the slope shown here, make each one about half as long again as the width of the front wall of the building. Cramp (clamp) each pair together temporarily at the apex, stand it on top of the wall panels (with the aid of a helper) and mark the positions of the notched cut-outs that will enable each rafter to rest on top of the wall panels. Cut the notches and the apex angles, secure the apex joint with corrugated fasteners (diagram 3), and nail each pair to the wall

panels (diagram 4). Add purlins as shown in diagram 5 to stiffen the structure; note that these extend beyond the front and rear walls to form the overhanging gables.

5 Nail on the plywood roof panels, fill in the gable wall ends with sections of clapboarding and add the gable endboards at each end of the roof. Cover the roof surface with roofing felt or shingles.

6 Finish the building by adding the door and glazing the windows. Tack beading around the openings to form rebates for the Plexiglas window sheeting and to act as a stop bead against which the door will close.

Below: *The steep pitched roof of this playhouse provides ample headroom for the occupants inside.*

A TRADITIONAL COUNTRY COTTAGE

This charming country cottage is a pretty fairy-tale confection finished in pink and white, with a delicate fenced porch at the front. It provides the perfect setting for those more domesticated children to play their own version of happy families.

Materials

Use only metric measurements for complete accuracy; the imperial measurements are given only as an *approximate* conversion.

The deck structure

2 x 2.1 m x 100 mm x 25 mm (6 ft 10 in x 4 in x 1 in) outer floor supports A1
2 x 1.96 mm x 100 mm x 25 mm (6 ft 5 in x 4 in x 1 in) inner floor supports B1
2 x 1.338 mm x 100 mm x 25 mm (4 ft 5 in x 4 in x 1 in) end floor supports C1
21 x 1.52 m x 100 mm x 25 mm (6 ft x 4 in x 1 in) floorboards D1
1 x 870 mm x 100 mm x 25 mm (2 ft 10 in x 4 in x 1 in) step E1
4 x 1.1 m x 75 mm (3 ft 7 in x 3 in) diameter short support posts F1
2 x 1.6 m x 75 mm (5 ft 3 in x 3 in) diameter long support posts G1
2 x 1.38 m x 50 mm x 25 mm (4 ft 6 in x 2 in x 1 in) front porch rails H1
2 x 730 mm x 50 mm x 25 mm (2 ft 5 in x 2 in x 1 in) side porch rails H2
22 x 470 mm x 50 mm x 25 mm (18½ in x 2 in x 1 in) porch palings J1

The wall panels

2 x 1.52 m x 38 mm x 25 mm (6 ft x 1½ in x 1 in) gable wall base rails A
2 x 450 mm x 38 mm x 25 mm (1 ft 6 in x 1½ in x 1 in) center cross rails B
4 x 1.29 m x 38 mm x 25 mm (4 ft 3 in x 1½ in x 1 in) gable wall inner posts C
4 x 890 mm x 38 mm x 25 mm (2 ft 11 in x 1½ in x 1 in) gable wall roof ledgers D
4 x 934 mm x 38 mm x 38 mm (3 ft 1 in x 1½ in x 1½ in) gable wall end posts E
8 x 918 mm x 38 mm x 25 mm (3 ft x 1½ in x 1 in) side wall posts F
4 x 1.24 m x 38 mm x 25 mm (4 ft 1 in x 1½ in x 1 in) side wall base/top rails G
4 x 480 mm x 38 mm x 25 mm (1 ft 7 in x 1½ in x 1 in) side wall window rails H

The wall covering, or clapboarding

12 x 1.3 m x 100 mm x 19 mm (4 ft 3 in x 4 in x ¾ in) long side wall covering 1
24 x 410 mm x 100 mm x 19 mm (1 ft 4 in x 4 in x ¾ in) short side wall covering 2
26 x 535 mm x 100 mm x 19 mm (1 ft 9 in x 4 in x ¾ in) door wall covering 3
13 x 440 mm x 100 mm x 19 mm (1 ft 6 in x 4 in x ¾ in) door covering 4
13 x 1.52 m x 100 mm x 19 mm (6 ft x 4 in x ¾ in) long rear wall covering 5
2 x 1.3 m x 100 mm x 19 mm (4 ft 3 in x 4 in x ¾ in) gable wall covering 6
2 x 1.5 m x 100 mm x 19 mm (3 ft 6 in x 4 in x ¾ in) gable wall covering 7
2 x 750 mm x 100 mm x 19 mm (2 ft 6 in x 4 in x ¾ in) gable wall covering 8
2 x 500 mm x 100 mm x 19 mm (1 ft 8 in x 4 in x ¾ in) gable wall covering 9
2 x 200 mm x 100 mm x 19 mm (8 in x 4 in x ¾ in) gable wall covering 10

The roof structure

2 x 1.21 m x 38 mm 25 mm (4 ft x 1½ in x 1 in) ridge boards J
4 x 1.08 m x 25 mm x 25 mm (3 ft 7 in x 1 in x 1 in) roof edge battens O
4 x 1.04 m 25 mm x 25 mm (3 ft 5 in x 1 in x 1 in) triangular roof edge fillets T
4 x 1.18 m x 100 mm x 25 mm (3 ft 11 in x 4 in x 1 in) gable end boards U
2 x 1.53 m x 100 mm x 25 mm (5 ft 1 in

Above: *This wooden-clad playhouse will provide hours of fun. Raised off the ground, it should be good for all-year-round play.*

x 4 in x 1 in) eaves boards V
2 x 1.53 m x 1.1 m x 19 mm (5 ft 1 in x 3 ft 8 in x ¾ in) roof panels X
2 x 410 mm x 120 mm (1 ft 4 in x 5 in) plywood support triangles

The door, windows and trims

4 x 470 mm x 38 mm x 25 mm (1 ft 7 in x 1½ in x 1 in) window horizontals K
4 x 404 mm x 38 mm x 25 mm (1 ft 4 in x 1½ in x 1 in) window verticals L
2 x 968 mm 38 mm x 25 mm (3 ft 2 in x 1½ x 1 in) door verticals M
2 x 440 x 38 mm x 25 mm (1 ft 6 in x 1½ in x 1 in) door horizontals N
4 x 404 mm x 25 mm x 25 mm (1 ft 4 in x 1 in x 1 in) window glazing bars (muntins) P
8 x 480 mm x 12 mm x 12 mm (1 ft 7 in x ½ in x ½ in) window stop beads Q
4 x 980 mm x 50 mm x 50 mm (3 ft 3 in x 2 in x 2 in) wall corner trims R
2 x 1.05 m x 50 mm x 12 mm (3 ft 4 in x 2 in x ½ in) door trim sides S1
1 x 580 mm 50 mm x 12 mm (1 ft 11 in x 2 in x ½ in) door trim top S2
2 x 434 mm x 434 mm x 3 mm (1 ft 5 in x

1 ft 5 in x ⅛ in) PVC window sheeting Z

Pegs
Nails
Metal angle brackets
Screws
Bituminous adhesive
Roofing felt
Roofing nails
Metal corner brackets
Step brackets
Hinges
Door and window latches
Paint

As an alternative to using a concrete base, the cottage is built on rot-resistant hardwood stilts to keep rising damp out of the

structure. Once these have been driven into position, the floor deck is hung from them and the walls are added in the same way as for the Scandinavian chalet. Two angled ridge boards support the roof panels, and the gable ends are finished with attractively shaped barge boards. Outward-opening side windows, a front door and the neatly-fenced verandah complete the building.

The materials list on pages 52-53 identifies the various components and gives detailed dimensions for building the house shown in the main photo. You can if you wish vary the dimensions to suit your family's requirements, but you should aim to maintain the floor joist and wall stud spacings used for this design to ensure its strength and stability.

Assembly

1 Mark out the site carefully with pegs and tape measure, check that everything is square (diagonal measurements should be equal) and then drive in the sharpened hardwood stakes with a sledgehammer (photo 1). Check that they are vertical with a spirit level. Cut all the stakes a little over-long to allow for their top ends to be trimmed level with each other when they have been driven in.

4

7

5

2 Clamp the two outer floor supports A1 to the inner faces of the posts with their top edges about 300 mm (12 in) above ground level. Use a spirit level to set them precisely level, and nail them to the posts (photo 2).

3 Secure the two end floor supports C1 between the outer floor supports A1. Then fit the two inner floor supports B1 between the end floor supports (photo 3).

4 Cut off the excess length from the four short support posts F1, and shorten the two longer posts G1 so that they project above the top edges of the floor supports by 500 mm (20 in).

5 Nail the floorboards D1 to the floor supports (photo 4). Notch the last one to fit

around the long support posts at the front edge of the verandah.

6 Place together the various frame members for the four wall panels, angling their ends as necessary, and nail them securely (photo 5). Reinforce the joint between the gable wall roof bearers with a metal angle bracket.

7 Tack the various lengths of wall clap-boarding to the wall panels in the correct sequence, working from the bottom edge

6

8

9

Template for repeat pattern

11

the wall panels and screw them to the ridge boards (photo 10). Nail them to the tops of the wall panels all round.

12 Pin the barge (gable end) boards U to the sloping edges of the roof, then stick the lengths of roofing felt in place with bituminous adhesive, running them up one side of the roof, over the ridge and down

hinge each window in place. Cut pieces of rigid PVC sheet to size and pin them to the insides of the windows. Add the door cladding to its carcase, and hang the door in its opening.

14 Finish the cottage itself by adding the wall corner trims R, the door architrave trims S, the roof edge fillets T and the

upwards (photo 6). Trim off the excess in line with the gable wall framing.

8 Stand the rear wall panel and one side wall panel on the floor, screw them together through the corners of the side posts and then screw each panel down to the floor (photo 7). Repeat with the other panels to complete the walls.

9 Nail the two ridge boards J to their two plywood support triangles Y, then hold the completed assembly in position and screw the triangles to the gable wall frame members (photo 8).

10 Mark out the repeat pattern on the edges of the gable end boards and eaves boards using the template (diagram 11), and cut it with a jig saw (photo 9).

11 Tack the roof edge battens O to the sloping edges of the plywood roof boards X. Then lay the boards in place on top of

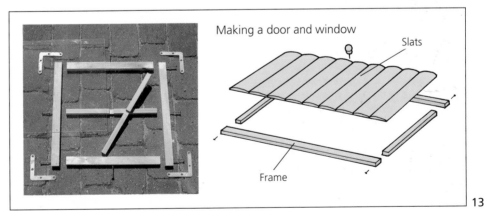

Making a door and window

Slats

Frame

13

the other side (photo 12). Leave an overlap at the eaves, which will be concealed behind the eaves boards V later.

13 Make up the windows and the door (diagram 13). Reinforce the corners of the windows with metal corner brackets fixed to their inner faces, tack the window stop beads round each window opening and

eaves boards V. Fence the porch by attaching the front and side rails H1 and H2 in place and nail on the palings J1.

Complete the assembly by fitting the step E1 on a pair of sturdy metal brackets, and add door and window latches.

Now all you have to do is paint the house and hand it over to its eager and no doubt, excited, new owners!

A GRASS-ROOFED PLAYHOUSE

If you want to build a playhouse with a difference, try one with a turf roof. It is certainly unusual to look at, yet has the major advantage of blending unobtrusively into the background in any yard.

Materials
Hardcore
Concrete
100 mm - 150 mm (4 in - 6 in) diameter rustic poles for wall clapboarding
76 mm x 76 mm (3 in x 3 in) lengths of sawed softwood for wall plates
76 mm x 50 mm (3 in x 2 in) lengths of sawed softwood for rafters
25 mm x 25 mm (1 in x 1 in) roof battens
Roofing felt
Turf
Nails

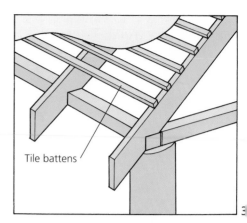

Tile battens

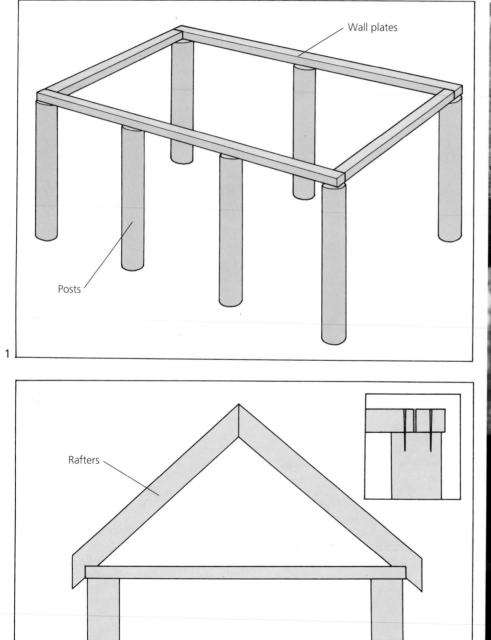

Wall plates

Posts

1

Rafters

2

The walls of this playhouse are covered with split poles to further enhance its rustic appearance....but only up to waist level, ensuring that its occupants can keep a sharp lookout in any direction. Its scale is child-size, but you could easily enlarge its dimensions for use as a summerhouse for all the family to enjoy.

The turf roof is really a novelty that will work best only in temperate climates, and even then will need regular watering with a garden hose to keep it green and healthy. If possible, site the building in a relatively shady area so that the turf does not dry out too quickly. Of course, there is no compulsion to install a 'green' roof; you could use roofing felt, shingles or tiles, if you prefer the building to have a more traditional appearance.

Building the playhouse

1 Embed the series of stout de-barked poles in the ground in concrete. There is a post at each corner of the building, one in the center of the rear wall and two (framing the door opening) in the front wall. Each post must reach up to the level of the eaves (diagram 1).

2 Link the posts along the front and back of the building with the wall plates. Space pairs of rafters about 600 mm (2 ft) apart and notch them over the wall plates (diagram 2); those at the ends of the building are blocked in with lengths of split poles to form solid gable ends.

3 To support the roof covering, nail the square battens to the rafters at 50 mm (2 in) spacings (diagram 3). Cover the rafters with roofing felt. The turf is laid on top of the felt; its weight keeps it safely in place. If you decide to use tiles or shingles instead of turf, space the battens a little wider and nail the individual tiles/shingles to them, in the same way as you would for a conventional roof.

4 The walls of the building are simply covered with lengths of split rustic pole, nailed to the outside of the support posts. The clapboarding at the ends of the building is attached first, then the front and

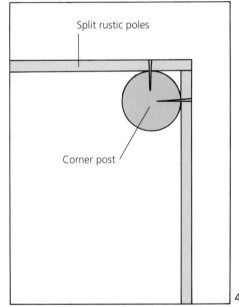

Split rustic poles

Corner post

4

back walls are treated in similar fashion with the poles neatly overlapping the ends of those on the end walls (diagram 4).

5 Give all the woodwork a generous brush coat of preservative to guard against rot and insect attack, and treat it with a fresh coat of preservative each year to keep it looking good (see page 10).

Left: *An unusual grass-roofed playhouse, with clapboarding built up to waist height to encourage lots of games. When it is dry, the turf will need to be hosed down occasionally.*

INDIVIDUAL PLAYHOUSES

If you have a big family or your children have a large circle of friends, a single playhouse may lead to endless squabbles and serious overcrowding. Here is an alternative that could have considerable appeal: individual playhouses for all!

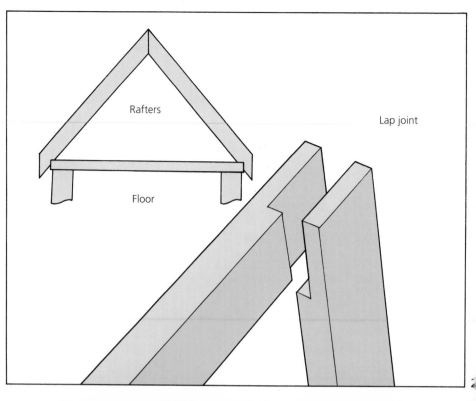

Materials

5 x 100 mm (4 in) diameter short stakes, approximately 760 mm (2 ft 6 in) long
Floor frame to fit from sawn timber
Floorboards or square of exterior-quality plywood
4 x 76 mm x 25 mm (3 in x 1 in) sawed softwood rafters
1 x 76 mm x 25 mm (3 in x 1 in) sawed softwood ridge board
Series of feathered-edge boards to clad roof and fill back wall
1 x horizontal board to cover top edge of roof
Nails

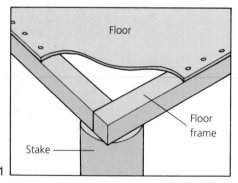

Each playhouse is big enough to be home to one average-sized child (or two smallish ones), and apart from giving all of them their own den, the structures are ideal for all sorts of games since they are easy and safe to climb.

Each one is built off the ground to keep dampness at bay, and can have its own optional front deck. The framework uses off-the shelf sawed timber, and the roofs are simply covered with preservative-treated fencing boards – the type used for making close-board fencing – so they are both durable and weatherproof (see page 10).

Making the playhouses

Each playhouse is based on a square floor plan, and can be built using a variety of timber off-cuts for economy.

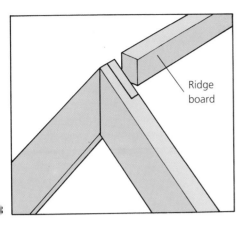

Ridge board

1 Start by driving a short sharpened stake into the ground at each corner of the building, and then saw the tops of the four stakes off about 300 mm (12 in) above ground level.

2 Make up the simple floor frame to rest

Below: *This group of simple shelters will help to prevent squabbles in a large family.*

squarely on top of the four stakes, and nail on the floorboards or a square of exterior-grade plywood (diagram 1). Secure the floor to the tops of the stakes by driving long nails down through the corners of the floor frame into them.

3 Link each pair of rafters in an A-shape by cutting simple lap joints where they meet at the roof apex. Nail the bottom ends of each pair of rafters to the edges of the floor deck (diagram 2).

4 Fix a ridge board between the front and rear rafter pairs (diagram 3). Then nail the fencing boards to the rafters, beginning at the eaves and working upwards towards the ridge (diagram 4). Top the roof off with a horizontal board nailed on to cover the upper edges of the topmost boards on each side of the roof slope.

5 Fill in the back wall with horizontal lengths of feathered-edge board. Angle their ends to match the roof slope and nail them to the face of the rear rafter pair.

6 Build the triangular aprons in front of each playhouse by driving in another stake in line with the center of the building. Then nail three boards on edge to this stake and to the two supporting the playhouse floor, and top them with decking boards cut to match the outline of the triangle. Leave a slight gap between the boards so that rain-water can drain between them.

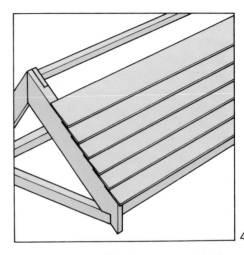

4

FORTS AND CASTLES

History and folklore are full of tales about castles housing cruel kings and beautiful princesses, and forts providing the settings for epic battles between the forces of good and evil. Children like nothing better than to be able to recreate their own versions of adventures they have read about or seen at the movies or on television, and here you can make their dreams a reality.

can be decorated with anything from shields to totem poles to add a touch of realism. Lastly, do not forget the essential feature of any self-respecting fort or castle: the flagpole.

Raw materials

The basic essentials for building a fort or castle are sturdy corner posts – either debarked tree trunks between 100 mm and 150 mm (4 in to 6 in) in diameter if you can get hold of a supply locally, or square sawed timber otherwise. What you use for

The major prerequisite for any half-decent castle or fort is commanding height. That does not mean you have to build on a huge scale; only that the top of the castle must put its occupants somewhere above adult head height! This means at the very least providing one raised platform which can serve as a lookout or a hideout, plus some means of access to it – ideally an attached ladder or ramp for safety's sake. If you can run to two storeys, so much the better; downstairs can then be the dungeon or the banqueting hall, the store room or the ammunition dump, depending on which particular scenario the children decide to act out.

It goes without saying that whatever

Above: *This fort has a ramp up to a walkway for 'defense'. A higher level platform should be added only for older children.*

you construct must be well built. As with so many outdoor play structures, the simplest method to use is the corner post technique, with the structure being built up around sturdy posts set in concrete. You can then bolt or screw floor and wall supports to the posts, add on wall covering to form palisades and castellations or create individual compartments within the structure. Raised platforms within the walls create battlements which can be reached by ramp or internal ladder, and the walls the rest of the structure depends on your budget and your ingenuity; you can spend a fortune at your local timber suppliers, raid your own scrap wood stockpile or go scavenging in the woods. If you can get hold of them, timber pallets – the platforms used for loading and unloading a wide range of goods using fork lift trucks – provide a particularly good source of suitable wood for both framing and covering. Whatever you use, remember that your children will be just as happy with a building that is purely functional; they do not need it to win design awards to enjoy playing in it, since their fertile imagination can create all the reality they need.

Built-in safety

Any structure with a raised platform must have guard rails of some sort to prevent accidental falls, and solid walls are by far the safest solution. Make them at least as high as the likely occupant's chest level, with vertical rather than horizontal clapboarding to discourage climbing on the inside or outside.

Pay particular attention to the design of any ladders used for access to the upper parts of the structure. Steps and rungs should be of planed or rounded timber to lessen the risk of splinters in hands and knees, and rungs must be securely fastened to prevent accidents. Attach handrails where possible to sloping external ladders, and always ensure that the ladder is securely and permanently fastened to the building at the top. For extra safety, peg the foot of the ladder at ground level too.

Involve the children

Building a fort or castle is the perfect opportunity to involve your children in its construction. You should of course keep strict personal control of potentially dangerous operations such as cutting wood to length, but you will find extra pairs of hands very useful for holding things in place as the construction proceeds, and if you spend a little time on some basic instruction you will soon have your helpers happily nailing on wall panels and tightening up nuts and bolts. They will certainly feel a great sense of pride at having been involved in even the smallest way, and their ideas will help you to create exactly the building they want.

Left: *This look-out style fort was built mainly from timber off-cuts and so cost very little.*

Below: *This open-topped fort was also constructed mainly from salvaged materials, such as old floorboards and doors. Only the four main supporting posts are new.*

A SIMPLE FORT

This simple square fort is easy to construct and makes the perfect playground for cowboys or crusaders, yet it could just as well be the fairy-tale castle where beautiful Rapunzel let down her hair or the Lady of Shalott eyed her mirror.

Materials
Hardcore
Concrete

4 x 100 mm - 150 mm (4 in - 6 in) diameter sturdy corner posts from rustic poles or sawed timber
100 mm x 38 mm (4 in x 1½ in) horizontal rails
100 mm x 38 mm (4 in x 1½ in) intermediate joists
Floorboards from rustic poles or sawed timber
Wall covering from rustic poles or sawed timber
Ladder made from planed timber

Ramps: from sawed or planed timber
4 x side ledgers
Slats
Slim battens
2 x horizontal braces

Nuts and bolts
Screws

Above: *This simply-constructed square fort could just as well be a fairy-tale castle.*

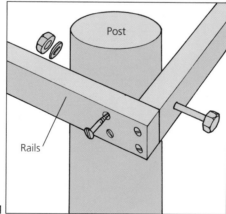

A straightforward design, this easily-constructed fort is built around four corner posts which are linked by sturdy horizontal rails at four levels to create a two-storey structure with endless play potential. The ground floor is raised, providing an inviting crawl space underneath, and is reached by two ramps. An internal ladder allows easy access to the upper floor, which has smartly castellated walls all round. The wall slats are spaced slightly apart to reduce wind resistance and allow some light into the ground-floor compartment.

Building the fort
Select a level, dry site, and mark out the positions of the four corner posts. The fort shown is about 2.4 m (8 ft) square and roughly 3 m (10 ft) high, but you can adapt the dimensions and the overall scale as you wish. Assemble all your tools and materials, ready to start work.

1 For a structure of this height, you need to set the corner posts in the ground to a depth of about 900 mm (3 ft). Dig each hole to a slightly greater depth, pack the bottom of the hole with some broken brick or similar material to assist drainage around the foot of the post, and stand it in place. Brace it upright with some scrap timber, pack in more rubble around its base and then fill the hole with concrete. Leave it to harden for about 72 hours before starting the fort construction.

2 Start attaching the horizontals to the outsides of the posts, using screws or nut and bolts. Set the first ones about 600 mm (2 ft) above ground level, and the next about 750 mm (2 ft 6 in) above; this second set of horizontals acts mainly to stiffen the structure, but also provides a fixing point for the clapboarding above the two ramp entry points. Add the third level about 450 mm (18 in) above the second level to form the upper floor, and fix the final level about 300 mm (12 in) down from the tops of the posts (diagram 1).

3 Add two intermediate joists at each floor level to prevent the boards from sagging, notching them into the perimeter horizontals. Board the ground floor first, then add two short joists to the first floor framework to form an opening for the ladder (diagram 2). Board the first floor next, trimming the boards around the opening.

4 Now you can start adding the clapboarding. Start at the corners, butt-joining the two boards in an L-shape. Nail on each length in turn, spacing the slats about 20 mm (¾ in) apart.To avoid wastage, butt-join lengths over the center of the main horizontal supports. Leave openings for access to the underfloor void at ground level and

for the two ramps that lead up to the ground floor itself. Form the castellations as you proceed around the fort, leaving alternate pairs of boards projecting above the level of the top horizontals.

5 Make up a sturdy ladder long enough to reach from the level of the ground floor to the top horizontals, set it in place in the

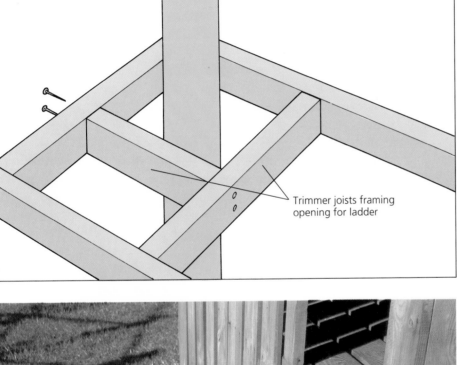

Trimmer joists framing opening for ladder

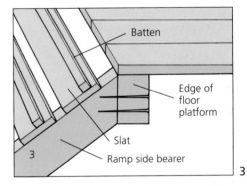

Batten

Edge of floor platform

Slat

Ramp side bearer

opening you created in step 3, and secure it to the fort walls.

6 Finish off by making up the two ramps that lead up to the ground floor. Nail the slats to two angled side ledgers, then make them slip-proof by nailing a batten to each slat (diagram 3). Set each ramp in place against the structure and nail it securely to the edges of the ground floor platform. Finally, add a horizontal brace to each ramp between the fort wall and the lower end of one of the ledgers for extra support.

7 Check that all fastenings are secure, and pound in all nail heads for safety. Then give the fort a coat of wood preservative (see page 10) and hand it over to its new owners.

DUAL-PURPOSE PLATFORM

A basic box construction with a drawbridge and a raised floor platform inside, this design has interchangeable front wall panels that can be removed and replaced in minutes, turning a fort into a Disney-style fairy castle – or whatever your children want.

Materials

From 18 mm (¾ in) exterior-grade MDO (medium density fiberboard) or plywood
1 x 2.44 m x 1.22 m (8 ft x 4 ft) back panel
2 x 1.22 m x 1.22 m (4 ft x 4 ft) side wall panels
1 x 1.525 m x 915 mm (5 ft x 3 ft) door panel
4 x 2.13 m x 760 mm (6 ft 11¼ in x 2 ft 6 in) interchangeable front wall panels
1 x 1.22 m x 760 mm (4 ft x 2 ft 6 in) drawbridge
1 x 2.44 m x 1.22 m (8 ft x 4 ft) floor panel

Cut the other timber components to fit from 50 mm x 50 mm (2 in x 2 in) square sawed softwood

Screws
Bolts and wing nuts
Hinges for drawbridge
Nylon rope for drawbridge
Plastic containers for counterweights
Flagpoles (optional)
Paint

Cut all components to size, then label them according to the materials list. If you are using plywood, sand the cut edges smooth.

Assembly

1 Mark out the crenellations on the top edges of the back and side walls, the front door panel and two of the inter-changeable front wall panels. Their precise dimensions are a matter of personal choice; those shown in the photographs were about 250 mm (10 in) wide and about 150 mm (6 in) deep. Cut them out and sand their edges smooth. Cut the tops of the other two interchangeable front wall panels to resemble turreted roofs.

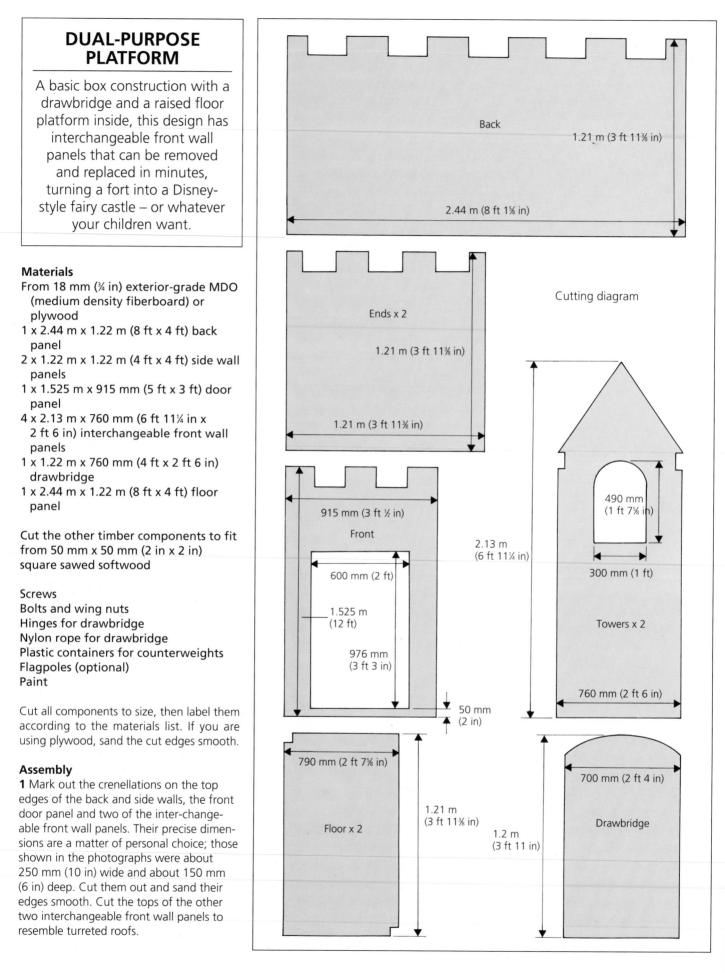

Cutting diagram

2 Mark and cut out the entrance on the front panel, creating an opening about 610 mm (2 ft) wide and 970 mm (3 ft 2 in) high which will be blocked off by the draw-bridge.

3 Mark out the window openings in the front wall panels. The fort walls should have narrow openings for archers, while the fairy-tale castle can have wider windows. Cut them out with a jig saw after drilling a hole within the waste area to admit the saw blade. Sand all cut edges.

4 Screw a corner post to each vertical edge of the two side wall panels. Then attach

Above: *A series of horizontal rails create the internal structure of the fort.*

three horizontal rails to each panel between the corner posts – one at ground level, one 610 mm (2 ft) above ground level to support the floor and one just below the crenellation – by driving screws through the panel into the rail behind.

5 With the aid of a helper, you can assemble the basic box structure. Secure the back wall panel to the two side walls by driving screws through it into the corner posts you attached in step 4. Then add horizontal rails to the back wall panel as you did for the side walls, with one at ground level and another 610 mm above ground level.

6 Cut two more long rails to size to run the width of the building. These link the front corner posts and support the three front wall panels. Fix them in place and then screw the front door panel to them, leaving equal spaces to the left and right for the interchangeable wall panels to be fitted.

7 Add vertical battens along each side of

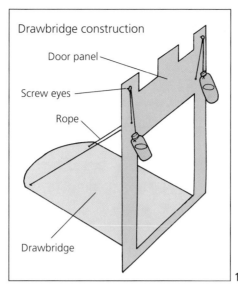

Drawbridge construction

Door panel

Screw eyes

Rope

Drawbridge

1

the door panel between the top and bottom batten. Then add horizontal floor supports to the corner posts and back panel.

8 Make 50 mm (2 in) square cut-outs in two corners of each floor panel so they will clear the posts. Then, with the assistance of a helper, lower the panels into the building so they rest on the floor support rails. Screw down through the edges of the floor panel into the support rails.

9 Drill clearance holes in the top and bottom front rails for the bolts that will attach the interchangeable front wall panels. Two at the top and two at the

bottom will be enough; make sure that the ones in the top rail do not coincide with the window positions. Then position each interchangeable wall panel in turn and insert your drill bit through the clearance holes in the rails to drill matching holes through the panels. Attach one set of panels to the rails with bolts and wing nuts to complete the shell of the building.

10 Screw a hinge to the drawbridge and hinge it to the bottom of the front door panel at each side of the opening so it will fold up flush against the panel. Then drill two holes for the drawbridge rope in the front door panel, above the door opening, and two holes in the top corners of the drawbridge (diagram 1).

11 Let the drawbridge down and attach the lengths of nylon rope to it, with the knots on the outside. Take each rope up through the holes in the front door panel and on up to a screweye fixed as high as possible to the inside of the door panel. Attach them to plastic drinks containers filled with water to act as counterweights. Adjust the rope lengths and the weights of the bottles as necessary to raise and lower the drawbridge fully.

12 Decorate the outside to look like stonework, the drawbridge to resemble planking and add other decorative touches.

Below: *This castle can be altered by simply changing the two towers' design.*

SANDBOXES

Children love the seashore – especially a sandy beach, where they can dig and build to their heart's content. The trouble is that for many families the seaside is too far away for more than the occasional trip. The answer is to provide a bit of beach in your back yard, in the form of a sandbox, where they can play whenever they want. You can build one in several different ways, using a variety of materials to help it blend in well with the yard design.

Constructing a permanent sandbox in the yard is a simple do-it-yourself job, and also a good opportunity to practice your practical skills on a relatively simple project. It can be raised or sunken (the latter is even easier to construct than the former), and can be turned into an ornamental pond or plant holder once the children have grown up.

Siting sandboxes
There are two main points to take into

Above: *This novel sandpit has wheels, so it can be moved around the garden. If the children are playing alone move it so it can be easily seen from the house.*

consideration when you are deciding where to put your sandbox. The first is safety: if the occupants are very young, you really need to be able to keep an eye on them from the house, so having it in view from the kitchen or living room window is

the ideal answer.

The second is tidiness: sandboxes have a habit of spreading their contents over a fairly wide area, so surrounding the box with a hard surface such as paving or giving it a wide seat all around will make it easier to sweep up straying sand at the end of the day. Try to avoid putting it under a tree, where resin and bird droppings could fall on its occupants in summer (autumn leaves are not such a problem).

Sizing sandpits
If you plan a raised sandbox, aim to make the sides about 380 mm (15 in) high so even tiny tots can climb in on their own. Similarly, a sunken sandbox needs about the same depth of sand. As far as other dimensions go, it really depends on the size of your yard, but a practical minimum is about 1.2 m (4 ft) square. Make it bigger if you can.

Choosing materials
You can construct a sandbox in several ways, two of which are illustrated here. One is to set logs on end in the ground, butting them closely together to form a palisade round the sandbox area. The other is to use planed timber to build a sandbox in the form of a wooden box with extended sides that help to stop the sand straying and also act as a seat. Some more ideas for building sandboxes are shown on the following pages.

As far as sand is concerned, the best type is washed play sand or river sand, which is available from building materials suppliers. On no account use ordinary bricklaying (masonry) or concreting sand, which will stain clothes and hands horribly. If you live near the seashore, you may be tempted to collect some sackfuls of your local beach sand; this might technically amount to theft and in any case is also not recommended since beach sand will have a high salt content which can make little hands both sticky and sore.

You need enough sand to fill the sandbox to a depth of about 225 mm (9 in); if it is any deeper, a lot more will find its way out of the box over the sides. So for a sandbox 1.2 m (4 ft) square you will need about a third of a cubic metre (about ½ cu yd) of sand. Scale the figure up accordingly for larger boxes.

Do not forget to incorporate features to stop the sandbox from turning into a bog in wet weather, and to prevent local pets or wildlife from using it as a toilet (with potentially unpleasant consequences for your children's health).

To allow rainwater to drain through the sand bed, fill the base of the sandbox with about 50 mm (2 in) of coarse gravel, topped with a sheet of heavy-duty polyethylene that you have perforated with small holes every 100 mm (4 in) or so; an electrician's small screwdriver is ideal for this. The polyethylene layer also discourages would-be human moles from digging too deep into the sub-soil.

To cover the sandbox at night and to keep animals from using it as a toilet, make a matching wooden cover which can simply be lifted into place.

Building a simple sunken sandbox
Pick your site and mark out the extent of the excavation with pegs and string lines. Excavate to a depth of about 300 mm (12 in), cutting the sides neatly and keeping them as vertical as possible. Look out for buried water or drain pipes as you dig, and reposition the pit if you find any.

To line the walls of the sandbox area, you can drive in sharpened log stakes, butting them closely together to keep the sand in place and to stop the surrounding soil from collapsing into the pit. Alternatively, drive wooden stakes – roughly sharpened to a point by four saw cuts – into the ground around the edge of the sandbox at, say, 900 mm (3 ft) inter-vals, then cut a sheet of exterior-quality plywood into strips, and nail them to the stakes to form a box with its top edge just below ground level. Smooth off and tamp down the base of the hole, then add gravel and a polyethylene sheet, as described earlier. Finally shovel in the sand to the required depth.

Below: *This sandbox is suitable for very young children. As it is very close to the house it's a good idea to contain the sand by fixing a board around the edge; this will also double as seating.*

A RAISED SANDBOX AND SEAT

This attractive square sandbox is built above ground, and can be set on any firm level surface. It provides a comfortable seat all around which also helps to discourage the spread of sand to the surrounding area by providing a surface that can be swept easily.

Materials

Hardcore
Concrete
8 x 76 mm or 100mm (3 in or 4 in) sq sawed softwood corner posts
76 mm x 50 mm (3 in x 2 in) sawed softwood rails to link posts
150 mm x 19 mm (6 in x ¾ in) planed softwood planks to cover exterior
Exterior-quality plywood to line the sandbox walls
Short joists
Seat boards as wall covering
Gravel
Polyethylene sheeting
Sandbox sand

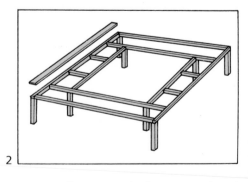

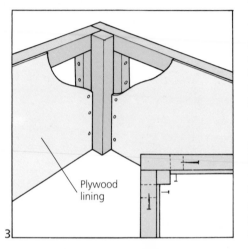

The sandbox is made from sawed and planed softwood. You can use the same boards you used for covering the ouside to line the walls of the sandbox itself, but 18-20 mm (¾ in) exterior-grade plywood would be more durable.

1 Start by deciding on the location and size of the sandbox. If the ground is relatively soft, you can simply drive the corner posts into the ground with a sledgehammer after sharpening them to a rough point with four saw cuts. Otherwise set each post in a hole dug to a depth of about 300 mm (12 in) and surround it with concrete. Check that the post tops are level, using a long timber straightedge and a spirit level.

2 Notch the tops of the posts as shown (diagram 1) to accept the support joists. To enable the wall covering to be attached later, these have to sit on edge with their faces flush with the post faces.

3 Nail the short joist sections between the joists along the two sides of the structure;

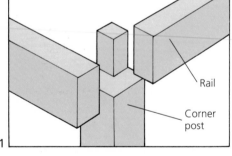

Plywood lining

this will be covered with planks running lengthwise (diagram 2). These short joists prevent the long boards from sagging.

4 Lay a 50 mm (2 in) deep bed of gravel beneath the sandbox area and cover it with polyethylene sheeting, perforated at intervals for drainage.

5 Line the walls of the box next, either with strips of plywood nailed to the posts and inner joists or with wall covering boards. Rest their bottom edges on the polyethylene sheeting (diagram 3).

6 Nail the wall covering boards to the sides of the outer posts and joists, to build up the external walls of the sandbox structure. Overlap their ends neatly at the external corners.

7 Nail the long seat boards in place to their supporting joists and to the post tops, then add the short lengths of board along the remaining two sides of the structure. For safety, pound in all the nail heads and smooth off any sharp or rough edges all around the seat area.

8 Fill the box with sand and get the buckets and spades ready.

Below: *This attractive sandbox has been constructed above ground and features a comfortable seat; this also helps to keep the sand off the surrounding lawn.*

A PATIO SANDBOX

This sandbox is constructed on three levels. The box itself is a square within a square; the inner part contains the sand, and is bounded by four triangular concrete slabs set in the corners of the larger square to form seats.

Materials
String and pegs to mark the site
Scrap timber for framework
Hardcore
Concrete

Bricks
Mortar
Plastic sleeve for umbrella (optional)
Gravel
Polyethylene sheeting

Timber to make square frame
Slats to make cover panels
Nails

This stylish sandbox combines a number of excellent design features in one simple project. The sandbox is in-ground, so construction is quite straightforward. It is surrounded by paving, which keeps the sand under control. The slot-in covers camouflage the sandpit when it's not in use, as well as keeping debris and wayward pets out of the sand. Lastly, an umbrella can be fitted to the center post to provide vital shade on hot, sunny days.

Assembly
1 Assuming that you are setting the sandbox into an existing patio that is laid over a sand bed, start by lifting some of the paving slabs or bricks to leave a square recess. Then mark out the central sandbox area with string lines and excavate the sand and subsoil to a depth of 450 mm (18 in).

2 Excavate the four triangular corner areas to a depth of about 200 mm (8 in), undercutting the edges of the surrounding paving by about 100 mm (4 in). Then peg timber formwork along their long sides and lay a 100 mm (4 in) thick bed of concrete in each corner. When it has set, mortar bricks into the gap between the concrete slabs and the underside of the surrounding paving to stop them from subsiding.

3 Cast a block of concrete in the centre of the sandbox square to support the inner corners of the slatted cover panels (diagram 1). Incorporate a plastic sleeve if you want to be able to use an umbrella.

Above: *An ingenious solution when space is at a premium – a sandbox by day reverting to adult use when the children are in bed.*

4 Cover the base of the sandbox square with gravel and a perforated polyethylene sheet and fill it with sand.

5 Make up the four cover panels by nailing slats diagonally to a square timber frame (diagram 2). Size the panels to match the dimensions of the outer sandbox square, and choose the dimensions of the frame timbers to match the depth between the top surface of the triangular concrete corner pads and the surrounding paving so that they sit flush with the patio surface.

Treat the panels with wood preservative to protect them from rot and insect attack (see page 10).

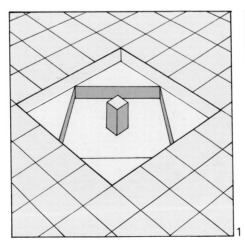

1

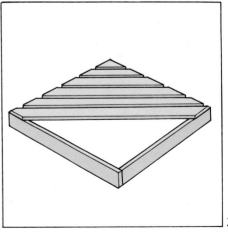

2

A SANDBOX AND TREE SEAT

This unusual sandbox and seat is designed to be built round a tree trunk, to provide both an attractive yard feature and a shady area for children to play and adults to sit and keep an eye on them. If you don't have a tree, don't worry! It can also be free-standing.

Materials

The dimensions given here are for making a structure 2.7 m (about 9 ft) long and 1.8 m (6 ft) wide. You can of course vary these dimensions if you wish. Use only metric sizes for complete accuracy; the imperial measurements are given only as an *approximate* conversion.

4 x 600 mm x 76 mm x 76 mm (2 ft x 3 in x 3 in) short stakes
4 x 900 mm x 76 mm x 76 mm (3 ft x 3 in x 3 in) long stakes
4 x 2.65 m x 152 mm x 25 mm (8 ft 7 in x 6 in x 1 in) side boards
4 x 1.8 m x 152 mm x 25 mm (6 ft x 6 in x 1 in) end boards

4 x 1.75 m x 152 mm x 25 mm (5 ft 9 in x 6 in x 1 in) cross boards
4 x 925 mm x 50 mm x 50 mm (3 ft x 2 in x 2 in) support ledgers
18 x 1.8 m x 152 mm x 25 mm (6 ft x 6 in x 1 in) decking boards
6 x 863 mm x 50 mm x 50 mm (2 ft 10 in x 2 in x 2 in) reinforcing battens

12 mm (½ in) thick exterior-grade plywood for lining sandbox
Gravel
Polyethylene sheeting
100 mm or 150 mm x 25 mm (4 in or 6 in x 1 in) wide planed boards for exterior vertical clapboarding
Nails

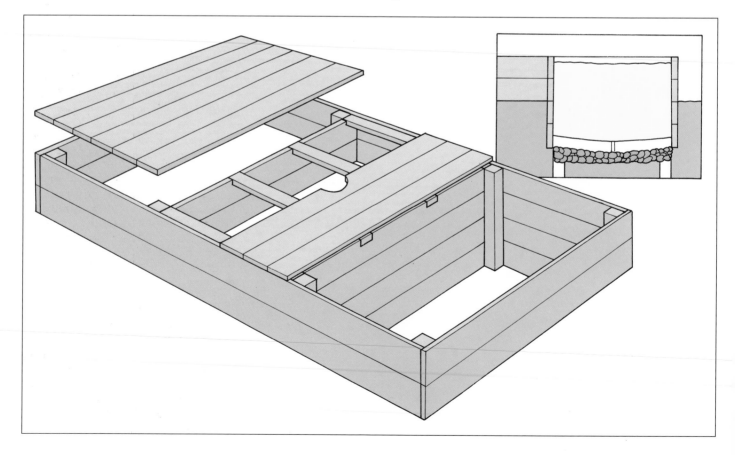

Left and Right: *Another example of a dual-use sandbox. This design even allows for parents to use half the sandbox cover for relaxing while their children play.*

Although this sandbox and seat are constructed around a tree trunk, a tree is not essential; the structure can be built on any reasonably level part of the yard.

It is built using a variation of the technique used for the above-ground sandbox featured on page 68. The structure is in three sections – the central portion with fastened decking around the tree trunk, one end section with a removable cover and some useful storage space beneath, and the other section dug out to form an in-ground sandbox, again with a removable cover (diagram 1). This design keeps the sand well below the tops of the sandbox walls, and so guarantees that most of it remains inside the box during even the most strenuous digging sessions.

Assembly

1 Start by setting out the site, marking the eight post positions with pegs. Then sharpen one end of each of the eight posts with four saw cuts. Drive them into the ground with a sledgehammer, checking that they are vertical and that their tops are level.

2 Excavate the hole for the sandbox to a depth of about 300 mm (12 in). You can either line the walls with exterior-grade plywood, fastened to battens nailed to the corner posts, or use flexible pond liner

stapled into place all around. The former will be more durable than the latter. Fill the base of the excavation with gravel and cover it with perforated polyethylene sheeting or more pond liner.

3 Nail the vertical areas of clapboarding to the posts as shown on page 70, overlap-

ping the external corners neatly, to create the three bays of the structure.

4 Fit the four support ledgers across the center bay to hold the fastened horizontal decking round the tree trunk. Cut notches 50 mm (2 in) wide 25 mm (1 in) deep in the top edges of the topmost vertical covering boards at each side of this bay, notch the ends of the four support ledgers and nail them into place.

5 Fix the horizontal decking to the central bay after making rounded cut-outs as necessary to allow the middle planks to fit around the tree trunk. Set the edges of the decking next to the storage area and sandbox back by 12 mm (½ in) from the edges of the vertical boards dividing the areas, so the side edges of the two removable lids can rest on the top edges of the vertical boards.

6 Make up the covers for the storage area and the sandbox by laying the decking boards side by side and nailing three reinforcing battens across the underside of each board. The two end battens should be inset from the ends of the cover boards by 100 mm (4 in), and all three should be inset from the sides of the boards by 25 mm (1 in) at one end and by 12 mm (½ in) at the other (diagram 1).

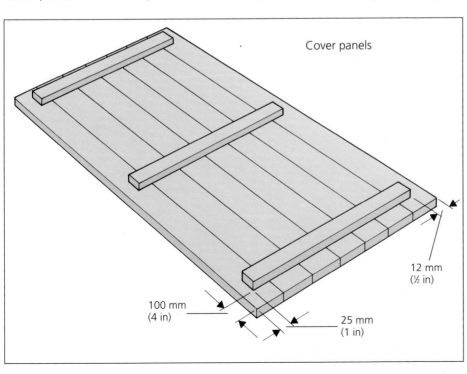

Cover panels

12 mm (½ in)

100 mm (4 in)

25 mm (1 in)

1

A RAISED PLAY TABLE

Construct a play table with a difference. This one is designed to hold water in one half and sand in the other. In this small landscape, children can dig and tunnel, make sand-castles or float boats and splash to their hearts' content.

Materials

From 18 mm (¾ in) exterior-quality plywood
2 x 1.464 m x 200 mm (4 ft 10 in x 8 in) box sides A
2 x 678 mm x 200 mm (2 ft 3 in x 8 in) box ends B

Below: *Designed for older children to enact some favorite games, this play table is also low enough for small children to enjoy.*

4 x 600 mm x 100 mm (2 ft x 4 in) leg faces C
4 x 600 mm x 82 mm (2 ft x 3¼ in) leg faces D
1 x 1.425 m x 678 mm (4 ft 7 in x 2 ft 3 in) table base E
1 x 675 mm x 145 mm x (2 ft 3 in x 5¾ in) divider F
4 x 400 mm x 50 mm x 50 mm (1 ft 4 in x 2 in x 2 in) softwood legs G
4 x 705 mm x 38 mm x 25 mm (2 ft 4 in x ¾ in x 1 in) softwood battens H
4 x 630 mm x 38 mm x 25 mm (2 ft x ¾ in x 1 in) softwood battens J
2 x 705 mm x 25 mm x 12 mm (2 ft 4 in x 1 in x ½ in) softwood trims K
2 x 630 mm x 25 mm x 12 mm (2 ft x 1 in x ½ in) softwood trims L

Optional table top

1 x 1.64 m x 890 mm x 18 mm (5 ft 4½ in x 2 ft 11 in x ¾ in) exterior MDF
2 x 650 mm x 25 mm 12 mm (2 ft 1 in x 1 in x ½ in) softwood battens to locate

Polyethylene sheeting
Woodworking adhesive

Screws
Heavy-duty staples
Panel tacks
Sandbox sand

Below: *With its top on, the sand and water table becomes an attractive and useful addition to your yard furniture.*

With this waist-level box, you can provide your youngsters with a raised sand tray for building and tunnelling, plus a small boating lake for all sorts of aquatic fun. The difference between this and a traditional ground-level sandbox or pool is that the children play while kneeling or standing around it, rather than climbing into it. There is ample room for several children to play together, and they will get just their hands wet and sandy, instead of being soaked and grubby from head to foot!

Making the play table

The table is made from 18 mm (¾ in) thick exterior-quality plywood, plus some softwood for the legs and support battens around the underside of the table surface. The table is lined with polyethylene sheeting or an off-cut of plastic garden pond liner, held in position with a softwood trim all around. All the fastenings are glued (make sure the woodworking adhesive is waterproof) and screwed for strength, and the resulting structure is both sturdy and handsome, especially if it is finished with brightly-colored wood stains. If you have an artistic bent, you could even paint some simple designs – a desert island, for example – on the sides of the box.

Dimensions

The dimensions for the components given in the materials list opposite make a play table that is 1.5 m (just under 5 ft) long, 750 mm (2 ft 6 in) wide and 600 mm (2 ft) high. You can vary these if you wish.

Use metric measurements for complete

Below: *The optional table top is easily put back and keeps the sand clean and dry.*

1

Above: *To drain water out use a simple fish tank siphon obtainable from most pet shops. Drain regularly in hot weather.*

accuracy; imperial measurements are given only as an *approximate* conversion.

Start by cutting out all the components and labelling them according to the materials list. Sand all their edges smooth so there is no risk of painful splinters.

Assembly

1 Make up the box walls by gluing and screwing the sides A and ends B together. Use three screws per joint.

2 Make up the four plywood leg assemblies by gluing and screwing parts C and D together in pairs. Fit five screws per assembly, spaced roughly 100 mm (4 in) apart.

3 Attach the leg assemblies to the corners of the box you put together in step 2, using glue and screws, so that the top edge of the box is level with the tops of the leg assemblies.

4 Glue and screw the table base support battens H and J to the inner faces of the box sides, level with their bottom edges.

5 Spread adhesive along the top edges of all the support battens. Then lower the table base E into the box so its edges rest on the battens, and drive screws down through the base into them. Then fit the divider F in place.

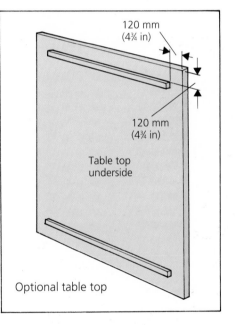

120 mm (4¾ in)

120 mm (4¾ in)

Table top underside

Optional table top

6 Glue one softwood leg G in place inside each leg assembly with its top touching the bottom edges of the base support battens. Drive screws through the leg assemblies into the legs for extra strength.

7 Cut the polyethylene sheet or pond liner to size and fold it neatly so that it will fit exactly inside the pool end of the play table. Then staple the edges and folds to keep it taut, and tack the trim battens K and L all around to neaten and conceal the top edges of the liner.

8 Stain or paint the table, then add sand and water and let the children loose!

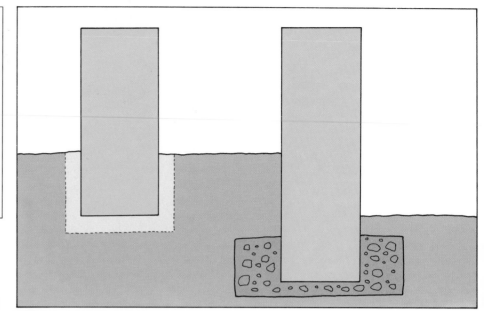

A LOG-LINED SANDPIT

This larger-than-usual sandpit is created with a series of logs, set close together to form a palisade. Not only does this keep the sand in, it also serves as seating. The size of the pit makes it suitable for more strenuous and adventurous activities.

Materials
String and pegs to mark out the site
Sawed logs 1 m x 150 mm - 230 mm (3 ft x 6 in - 9 in) in diameter
150 mm (6 in) long wire nails (optional)

If you have a relatively large yard, you might like to consider creating a play area a little larger than the traditional sandpit. This can then be used not only for all the usual digging and building activities, but also for dirt bike races, long jump competitions and anything else that a child's fertile imagination can dream up.

The main problem with a sandpit built on such a grand scale is the age-old one of keeping the sand where it belongs. Since the activities it is likely to host may well be rather more strenuous than building sandcastles, you really need a more substantial

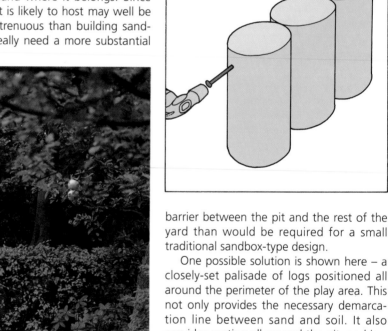

barrier between the pit and the rest of the yard than would be required for a small traditional sandbox-type design.

One possible solution is shown here – a closely-set palisade of logs positioned all around the perimeter of the play area. This not only provides the necessary demarcation line between sand and soil. It also provides seating all around the pit, and is a particularly good way of coping with sloping sites where the log palisade can, for example, hold back flower beds at a higher level than the pit itself.

Building the palisade
To build the palisade shown here you need a supply of sawed logs between 150 mm and 230 mm (6 in to 9 in) in diameter and each about 900 mm (3 ft) long.

Left: *The design possibilities for log-lined sandpits are endless and only governed by the size and shape of your garden.*

You may have to do some research in your area to locate the best source of such logs if you do not have access to a sawmill which specializes in poles. Firms removing tree-felling work are one option, and it may be worth contacting your local parks department; both need to dispose of felled trees and lopped branches and may be only too glad to supply your requirements.

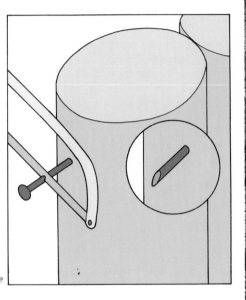

Logs of this size are heavy enough to stay in place without the need for any additional reinforcement – on level sites at least. If they are acting as retaining walls, however, you would be wise to lock them in position by bedding them in a trench filled with concrete (diagram 1).

1 On a level site, start by marking out where you want to site the log walls using pegs and string lines. Then dig a trench about 300 mm (12 in) deep along each marked line, spreading any topsoil you

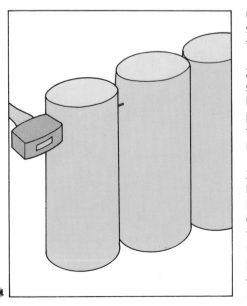

remove elsewhere on the garden and saving the subsoil for use as packing when the logs have been set in place.

2 Level the base of the trench and start standing the logs in place along the center line. Butt them together as tightly as possible to stop sand from leaching out through the gaps, and aim to get their tops roughly level with each other.

3 You can give the log wall extra stability by driving a wire nail into the side of each log to a depth of about 75 mm (3 in) (diagram 2). Then use a hacksaw to cut off the head of the nail, sawing through the nail shank at an angle to leave a sharp point (diagram 3). Offer up the next log and use a club hammer or small sledge-hammer to knock it on to the nail and lock

Above: *This larger-than-average sandpit will help keep the sand to one area of the garden. Put fresh sand in each summer.*

it securely to its neighbor (diagram 4). Repeat the process as you place successive logs in position.

4 Shovel subsoil around base of logs along both sides of trench, and use an off-cut of fence post or similar thick piece of wood to compact it down around them.

5 When you have completed building the palisade, clear vegetation and topsoil from within the pit area and compact the surface. Then dump in the sand, fill the pit to a depth of at least 230 mm (9 in) and rake it out ready for play to begin.

A COMBINED SANDBOX AND WADING POOL

A quick-to-assemble structure, this combined pool and sandbox can be dismantled at the end of the summer yet will provide your children with a season of fun. It is made from fairly basic materials – planed softwood and polyethylene sheeting or pond liner.

Materials
From planed softwood
4 x 150 mm x 25 mm (6 in x 1 in) perimeter boards
50 mm x 25 mm (2 in x 1 in) supports
38 mm x 25 mm (1½ in x 1 in) supports
2 x 150 mm x 38 mm (6 in x 1½ in) dividers

Sandbox cover:
38 mm x 25 mm (1½ in x 1 in) wood frame
19 mm (¾ in) square battens to reinforce frame
38 mm x 19 mm (1½ in x ¾ in) slats
3 x 38 mm x 25 mm (1½ in x 1 in) battens to reinforce slats

Screws
Polyethylene sheeting or pond liner
Staples or tacks
19 mm (¾ in) square battens to neaten pool edge
Sandbox sand

Most of the sandboxes in this section of the book are semi-permanent structures designed to last several summers – or at least until the children's 'sandbox' years have passed and they can be turned into an alternative yard feature such as a pond or planter. This design is intended to be far more temporary; it can be put together in an afternoon, and can be just as quickly dismantled at the end of the summer. All

Below: *The space between the sandbox and the wading pool helps to minimize the amount of sand that gets into the water.*

1

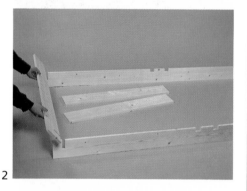

2

3

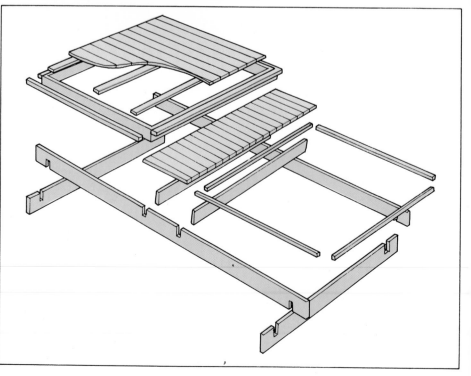

you need to erect it is a paved area of a reasonable size; the structure shown here is about 2.4 m (8 ft) long and around 1.2 m (4 ft) wide, but you can easily vary these measurements if you wish.

It also combines every small child's two favorite play materials, sand and water, in one compact structure. The box is divided into three bays, with the narrow central area serving not only as a useful storage box for buckets, spades and water toys but also as a divider between the two play areas; sand and water mix perfectly well at the seaside, but can make an awful mess in your back yard!

Assembly

The raw materials used to construct this pool are planed softwood in assorted sizes (see the materials list opposite for details) as well as some heavy-duty polyethylene sheeting or flexible pond liner for the wading pool.

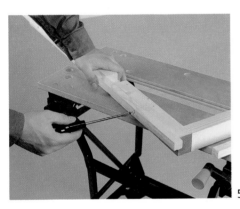

5

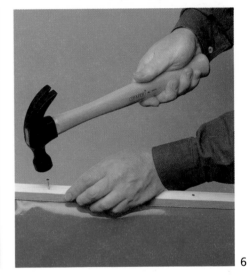

6

1 Mark out lap joints 75 mm (3 in) from the end of each of the perimeter boards to allow them to interlock in the same fashion as winebox dividers. Cut out the eight joints with a saw and chisel. They should be a tight fit when the boards are assembled.

2 Mark two cut-outs in the top edges of each of the long frame boards, each about 100 mm (4 in) away from the mid-point of the board, to accept the 38 mm (1½ in) supports for the decking boards. Cut the waste out with saw and chisel.

3 Mark the positions of the central dividers on the inner faces of the long frame boards, setting them about 380 mm (15 in) apart, and drill clearance and countersink holes for the screws at these points (photo 1).

4 Assemble the four main frame boards by interlocking their corner halving joints (photo 2). Then position the two dividers between the long frame boards and drive screws into their ends through the holes you made in the boards in step 3 (photo 3).

5 Make up the cover for the sandpit. Start by assembling the frame so it will just fit within the walls of the sandbox. To stop it dropping down inside the box, screw on slim square battens all round the edge of the frame, level with its top face, to form a lip (photo 4).

6 Attach the slats to the top of the frame you assembled in step 5, using a slat off-cut on edge as a spacer (photo 5). Then fasten the three support battens to the undersides of the slats, as shown in the

main diagram, to prevent them from sagging if the cover is walked on.

7 Attach the slats to the two 50 mm (2 in) decking supports. Space the supports to match the spacing of the cut-outs you made in step 2, and make the slats long enough to reach to the mid-point of the central dividers when the assembled boardwalk is laid in position over them. As in step 6, use a slat off-cut held on edge to space the slats out evenly.

8 Cut the polyethylene sheeting or pond liner to size to fit the wading-pool box and lay it in place, folding the internal corners neatly. Tack or staple it to the top edges of the box, then tack on lengths of 19 mm (¾ in) square batten all round to neaten and protect the edge (photo 6).

A SANDPIT FOR THE FUTURE

With a little forward thinking you can plan ahead when you build a sandpit. This design can be transformed into a flower bed or garden pond when its life as a play structure is over.

Materials
Coarse gravel
Polyethylene sheeting
Mortar
Cut stone
Builders' sand
Sandbox sand

Your children's demand for a sandpit will not last for ever, and there will come a time when their attentions will turn to more grown-up play activities. At that point it seems a pity simply to have to demolish whatever you created for them; a better solution is to design a pit that can easily be turned into another garden feature such as a flower bed or a garden pond, and the design shown here is a perfect example of this.

In its incarnation as a sandpit, it is a gently curved truncated heart shape set at the edge of a block-paved patio. The perimeter of the pit is finished off with a border of cut stone which neatly conceals the heavy-duty polyethylene sheet lining the excavation.

Assembly

1 To form a sandpit, dig out the shape to a depth of about 300 mm (12 in), keeping the sides of the excavation vertical. So long as the subsoil is firm and well-compacted, the sides should not need any additional reinforcement (diagram 1).

2 Excavate a narrow shelf all round the perimeter of the hole, wide and deep enough to allow the cut stone to be set in place on it in a mortar bed (diagram 2).

3 Then lay a 50 mm (2 in) deep bed of coarse gravel in the base of the excavation and drape the plastic sheeting over it. Tuck it into the sides, forming neat folds where necessary, and pierce it with holes at intervals across the base of the excavation so that water can drain through it into the subsoil (diagram 3).

4 Trim off excess material round the edge

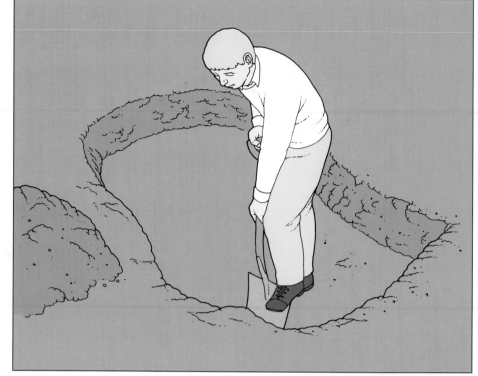

of the lining with scissors or a sharp knife so a narrow strip rests on the shallow perimeter shelf you cut in diagram 2.

5 Spread a bed of mortar on top of the lining all around and bed the cut stone into place, level with the surrounding paving (diagram 4). Point neatly between them, then fill the pit with sand to a depth that is just sufficient to conceal the lining.

Converting to a pond
When the sandpit's working life is over, you may decide to turn it into an ornamental pond instead.

To do this, you will first have to dig out the sand. Do not waste it, though; use

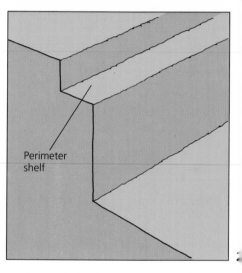

Perimeter shelf

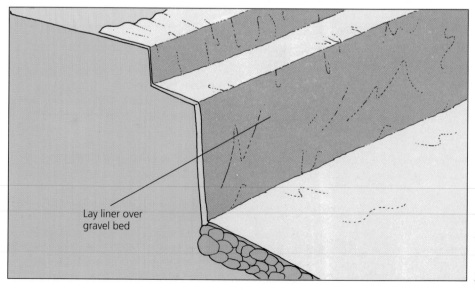

Lay liner over gravel bed

Above: *This sandpit can also be lined and used as a pond or a wading pool.*

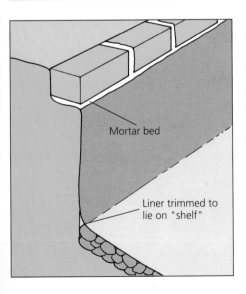

Mortar bed

Liner trimmed to lie on "shelf"

some as top dressing for the lawn, and dig the rest into your flower beds to improve the soil texture. Then carefully break away the cut stone and their bedding mortar all around the pit perimeter so you can remove the old lining.

The original hole is not really deep enough for a garden pond, especially if it is to contain fish. Dig out the gravel base you laid beneath the pit lining, and excavate the center part of the pit to a minimum depth of about 450 mm (18 in); 600 mm (24 in) would be better. Slope the sides of this deeper section gently, leaving a shallower shelf at the level of the original excavation on which to grow aquatic plants.

Line the excavation with damp sand and drape the new pool liner in place. Partly fill it with water and carefully pull out creases in the liner so it conforms to the outline of the excavation. Then trim excess material from the edge of the liner all round, as

described for lining the wading pool, and replace the perimeter setts on a fresh mortar bed to complete the conversion.

Converting to a flower bed

If you prefer to turn your redundant sandpit into a flower bed, you have a far easier job than the pond conversion described above.

Simply dig out the sand, then cut through the liner all round at the point where it disappears beneath the perimeter cut stone. Lift it out, but leave the gravel bed beneath it in position. Then fill the original excavation with good-quality soil and compost, ready for planting.

As an alternative to simply filling your unwanted sandpit with soil, you could turn it into a sunken rockery instead. Bed the rockery stones in place on the bottom of the pit, then add soil and fine gravel and plant it up with alpine plants.

SWIMMING POOLS

A swimming pool is no longer just a status symbol: it is a permanent health and leisure centre on your own doorstep, ready to be enjoyed by family and friends and the perfect focal point for parties, barbecues and the like. It is also eminently affordable, and few home improvements can be relied upon to give so much pleasure to so many for so long. Having one could completely change your lifestyle, and there is no doubt it will also enhance the value of your home.

What's available?

There are four main types of pool to choose from. At the bottom end of the price scale come the above-ground pools, which are designed to be erected from prefabricated components on any flat, level area. The walls usually consist of modular ribbed steel or reinforced glass fiber (fiberglass) sections that are locked together and fitted with a heavy-duty liner. They can usually be put up in a day and come in a range of shapes and sizes and can even be taken with you when you move. However, access can be difficult, especially for small children, who cannot always dive into them and they are hard to camouflage.

Next come variations on the first type, but designed for in-ground installation. The necessary excavation work obviously raises the price, but in-ground installation makes access to the pool far easier for everyone.

You can also obtain one- and two-piece fiberglass pools in a range of shapes and

Right: If you have a large pond or stream in your yard, a raft is a must. Attach it to the bank on a rope so it can be hauled in.

Below: This natural pool has a pool liner attached to the bottom to make access to the water easier.

sizes, delivered ready to be set in a prepared excavation. Installation of these pools is obviously extremely quick, but because of their size excellent access to the yard is essential.

At the top of the price range come in-ground concrete pools. Their walls are either built up from interlocking panels or reinforced blockwork, or are created by spraying concrete on to a reinforcing mesh (the gunite system), and are lined with mosaic tiles, marbleite (marble plaster) or similar materials to give a permanent waterproof finish. Prices obviously depend on size and site factors.

Natural water features

You may be fortunate enough to have a natural water feature in your yard – a stream or a spring, for example – which you can dam or turn into somewhere for your children to swim. Otherwise you will have to build a tailor-made pool from scratch. You can often carry out the assembly yourself, but you cannot do it successfully without the right components, fittings and accessories.

If you are making use of a natural water feature you have plenty of scope for making your own accessories. Two examples, shown here, are a landing/diving stage and a rope-operated raft.

Materials
Landing stage:
4 x metal fence spikes
4 x fence posts
4 x horizontal support beams
Planed timber decking slats

Raft:
Supporting logs
Split rustic poles or planed timber slats
Nylon rope or galvanized wire

Rust-proof screws or nails

Landing stage

1 The landing stage requires secure supports – two on land and two at the water end of the decking. The easiest way of providing these is to set the support posts in metal fence spikes driven in with a fence post off-cut and a sledgehammer. You can use sharpened stakes otherwise.

2 Then bolt four strong horizontal support beams in place between the post tops, butting their ends together.

3 Screw on the decking slats, spacing them slightly apart to allow water to drain between them. Use rust-proof screws for this, and countersink their heads into the slats for safety.

Raft

4 Bind the supporting logs together side by side with galvanized wire or rot-proof nylon rope to ensure the raft's structural integrity.

5 Cut the deck slats to length and nail or screw them securely to the logs. Pound in nail heads and countersink screws.

6 Tie a rope to each end of the raft and run the ropes to tie-off posts on the bank, so the rafters can pull the craft safely back and forth across the water.

Which one to choose?

Money is obviously the deciding factor when you are choosing which sort of swimming pool to have. However, an in-ground pool is undoubtedly the best investment because it allows you to enjoy a full range of aquatic and poolside activities, such as parties and barbecues.

The primary function you wish your pool to fulfil will determine the size and shape you choose. The first thing to remember is that you need to provide around 10 sq m (about 100 sq ft) of pool area for every user, so a family of four would need a 40 sq m (430 sq ft) pool – say a rectangle measuring 8 m x 5 m (about 26 ft x 16 ft),

or a circle about 7 m (22 ft 6 in) across. Finally, if you want to be able to dive in, you will need one end at least 2 m (6 ft 6 in) deep.

Allow an area at least 1 m (3 ft) wide around the pool for easy access, and cover it with a smooth, hard, non-slip surface that is easy to keep clean.

Rules and regulations

Regulations governing the construction of swimming pools vary from country to country. Ask your local authority what their requirements are when installing a swimming pool, and check with your local water supply company.

OUTDOOR EATING

Children love eating out of doors. Apart from the obvious sense of adventure that even the most impromptu picnic creates, a meal in the yard means freedom from grown-ups and an escape from having to remember their best table manners! They can eat with their fingers, lob half-eaten apple cores into the undergrowth with impunity and spill their drinks wherever they like. With a little adult super-vision, they could even have a camp fire.

Children will usually want to decide for themselves where they eat, probably choosing the most unlikely spots, but you can if you wish provide some tailor-made garden furniture for them to use – see overleaf for details.

An alternative approach is to encourage their sense of independence by providing them with their own barbecue pit, where they can learn the basic outdoor survival skill of setting and managing a fire – initially with some adult supervision – and can then be left to broil their hot dogs and hamburgers to their hearts' content. And if you are not yet ready to trust them with a real fire, you could still let them cook things using the much safer throwaway barbecue trays now widely available from supermarkets, hardware stores and garages. With the latter, all you have to do is light the charcoal and then make sure the children understand that what will sizzle their sausages is hot enough to burn their fingers too!

Building a barbecue pit
Materials
Cut stone or small paving blocks
Mortar
Sand

The most important factor in building any site for a fire is the danger to surrounding vegetation – and possibly to wooden yard items such as fences and garden sheds. A fire that is apparently under control can flare up unexpectedly, especially in windy weather, and it takes only a flash of flame to scorch shrubs, hedges and overhanging branches, or to ignite a dry wooden fence.

1 Start by selecting a site in the open, well out of harm's way – and ideally in view of the house, so you can keep a watchful eye on the proceedings without being too obtrusive.

2 Bare earth or a bed of sand is the best base for a fire. Never light one on solid paving, since the resulting black scorch marks will be impossible to remove. Mark out the area for the pit, making it as large as space allows. Then clear any vegetation from the area and dig down to a depth of about 150 mm (6 in) to form the pit.

3 It is a good idea to give the pit a fixed border, using for example cut stone or small paving blocks bedded in mortar to keep them in place around the perimeter. You can then lay paving up to the edge of the pit on a sand bed so the children have somewhere firm and dry to sit while they are tending their fire and doing the cooking (photos 1 and 2).

4 When the border stones are in place and the mortar has set, spread a bed of sand or sieved soil over the base of the pit ready for the first fire to be lit.

Fire safety in the garden
It is essential that an adult supervises children's first attempts at lighting a fire. Unless you want to show off your caveman skills with sticks and tinder, the safest way of starting a fire is with a lighter, lit with a match and then covered with small dry sticks. Once these have caught light, add thicker sticks and small dry logs, followed by larger ones once the fire is well lit. Avoid using wood fresh from the undergrowth near the ground, which will burn very

Right: *Nothing tastes so good as hot dogs cooked over your own fire, but this should only be allowed with older children.*

smokily. Unnecessary smoke will annoy your neighbors as well as getting in your children's eyes.

If the fire is to be used for cooking, you will get the best results by using a small quantity of smokeless fuel or charcoal rather than wood. Light the fire as described with a lighter and some sticks, then place a layer of the fuel over the sticks. Leave the fire for a while until the coals begin to glow before you start trying to cook anything.

Never use any flammable liquid such as gasoline to start a fire or revive one that is dying, and make sure your children understand this rule too. Many household chemicals and aerosols are flammable, and an aerosol can thrown into a fire could explode with potentially fatal results if anyone is nearby.

If the children want to cook things over a fire, make sure they have suitable tools – either proper cooking implements, perhaps borrowed from the family barbecue – or improvised ones otherwise. You can make an excellent toasting fork for such foods as hot dogs by using wire coathangers and wood off-cuts. Unbend the hanger and cut the wire in half with cutters or a small hacksaw. Then drill a hole slightly smaller in diameter than the wire in the end of a scrap of wood the right shape and size to act as a handle, and push the wire in. The wire will not taint the food, and the handle will protect fingers from the heat.

Lastly, as a safety precaution, always keep a large bucket of water handy near the fire so you can douse it quickly if it should get out of control. Show the children how to do this in case you are out of earshot, and tell them to use it in an emergency to cool burned fingers too.

Left: *This bare soil pit can also be used for barbecues or turned into a flower bed.*

YARD FURNITURE FOR CHILDREN

A set of children's yard furniture is simple and straight-forward to make, yet looks perfectly harmonious in any yard setting. Decorate the pieces with a microporous paint or use a proprietary wood stain.

Materials

12 x 1 m x 100 mm x 38 mm (3 ft x 4 in x 1½ in) wooden slats

6 x 50 mm x 38 mm (2 in x 1½ in) transverse ledgers

4 x 76 mm x 38 mm (3 in x 1½ in) timber table legs

8 x 63 mm x 38 mm (2½ in x 1½ in) timber bench legs

6 x 50 mm x 38 mm (2 in x 1½ in) short lengths of timber to fix transverse ledgers

75 mm x 38 mm (3 in x 1½ in) leg braces

Sandpaper
Exterior wood filler
Screws

This attractive set of scaled-down yard furniture is perfect for children's meals, and could not be easier to make. The table top and bench seats are simply planks of wood, set on sturdy X-frame legs to form a solid structure that is heavy enough to stay put even in high winds. They are both finished in microporous paint, which allows water vapor to pass through the paint film without causing the inevitable cracking and peeling that occurs with ordinary paints. This type of paint weathers by erosion, so redecorating is simply a case of washing down the existing paintwork and applying a fresh coat over the top. You can if you prefer use wood stain as an alternative decorative finish.

Assembly

1 Make up the table top first, cutting the components to the dimensions shown in the diagrams, to make a table measuring 1 m (3 ft 3 in) long, 600 mm (2 ft) wide and 600 mm (2 ft) high. The table top consists of six slats screwed to two transverse ledgers with a narrow gap between each slat to allow rain water to drain off easily.

2 Countersink the screw holes deeply and fill the recesses with exterior-quality wood

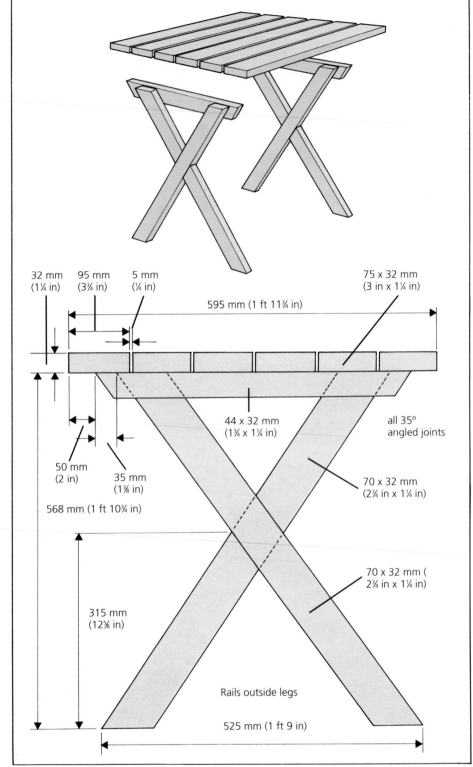

filler to remove any risk of rust showing through the paint finish. Ideally use galvanized or other rustproof screws.

3 Make up the bench seats in exactly the same way as the table top, using three slats per bench. Each bench is 1 m (3 ft 3 in) long, 350 mm (14 in) high and 295 mm (11½ in) wide.

4 Next, make up the table legs, joining them with a cross-lap joint at an angle of 60°. If you do not have a protractor and a sliding bevel to help you set out the angles, remember that all three sides of a triangle with 60° corner angles measure the same length, and use this to set the pieces at the correct angle. Cut the lap joints with a tenon saw and chisel, check their fit, then

drill through the joint and secure it with screws or, if you prefer, a coach (carriage) bolt and nut (diagram 1).

5 Make up the bench legs in the same way. Screw each leg assembly to the outer face of a transverse ledger beneath the table top or seat. Then screw a short length of wood to the underside of the top/seats, at right angles to each transverse ledger, to

which the diagonal leg braces will be attached (diagram 2).

6 Measure up the required length for each pair of braces, cut their ends at 45° angles, drill deep countersinks for the screws and fasten them in position.

7 Finish off by sanding down all the surfaces with sandpaper. Then paint or

Above: *A scaled-down set of yard furniture painted in bright colors will be a popular addition to the yard.*

stain each item ready for use. To avoid arguments between the children over who owns what, you could paint each seat a different color and even letter their names on the backs.

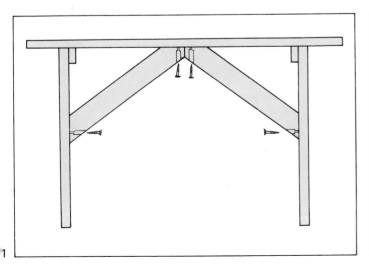

1

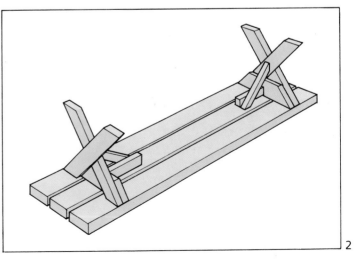

2

WEEKEND PROJECTS

Many of the projects in this book have been quite complex and time-consuming to put together. This final selection is on an altogether simpler level. Some projects will take no more than an hour to put together, providing a stunningly fast parental reaction to those vacation cries of "We're bored!". Others may take a little longer, but can still easily be built, decorated and handed over within a weekend.

A SAIL AWAY SANDBOX

This striking little craft is designed as a mobile sandbox on wheels, but can also become anything that floats – a pirate's galleon, a fishing boat or just a cargo ship sailing across the patio or the lawn.

Materials
From 16 mm (⅝ in) plywood
1 x 1.06 m x 720 mm (3 ft 5 in x 2 ft 5 in) A
2 x 1.5 m x 200 mm (5 ft x 8 in) B
2 x 720 mm x 295 mm (2 ft 5 in x 11½ in) C
From sawed softwood
4 x 750 mm x 102 mm x 25 mm (2 ft 7 in x 4 in x 1 in) D
2 x 1.35 m x 50 mm x 25 mm (4 ft 4 in x 2 in x 1 in) E
1 x 678 mm x 25 mm (2 ft 3 in x 1 in) diameter dowel F
4 x 70 mm x 40 mm x 4 mm (2¾ in x

1½ in x ⅛ in) plywood G
1 x 1.84 m x 690 mm (2 yd x 28 in) canvas for sail H
Woodworking adhesive
Screws
Wheels
Bolts, washers and nuts
Nylon/metal eyelets for sail
Narrow rope
Snap hooks
Screw eyes
Sandpaper
Sandbox sand

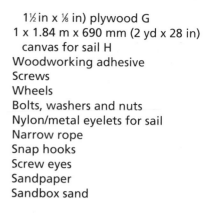

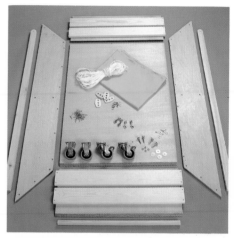

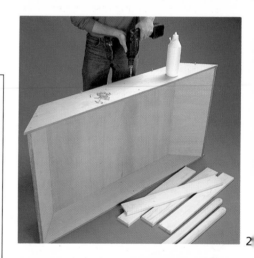

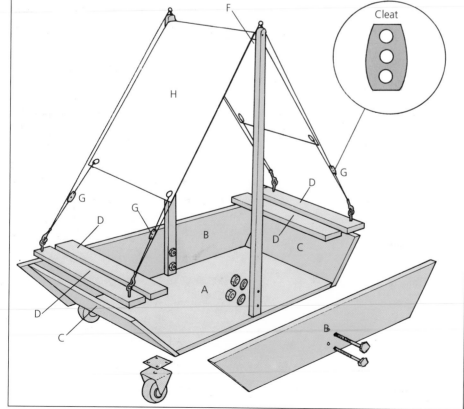

Cleat

Right: *This mobile sandbox will provide hours of imaginative play and can be towed to wherever you can keep an eye on the children.*

Use metric measurements for complete accuracy; imperial measurements are given as an *approximate* conversion.

Making the boat

1 Start by cutting the components to size and labelling them clearly. Note that the ends of part A and the long edges of parts C are cut at an angle of 45°, using a jig saw with an adjustable footplate (photo 1).

2 Assemble the hull by gluing and screwing parts B to the edges of part A, and then to the ends of parts C. Note that parts C are inset by 10 mm (⅜ in) from the sloping edges of parts B. Use 38 mm (1½ in) screws driven through clearance holes, and countersink and fill the screw heads (photo 2).

3 Glue and screw the four seat slats D to the ends of the boat. For extra strength, also drive screws up through parts C into the outer slat at each end of the boat (photo 3). Then attach the wheels by screwing their mounting plates securely to the underside of the boat.

4 Clamp the masts E to the sides of the boat and drill two holes through both components. Remove the clamps and attach the masts with bolts, washers and nuts (photo 4). Then round off the tops of the masts and screw the sail support F between them.

5 Cut the sail to size, hem it all round and fit a metal or nylon eyelet in each corner. You will need four cleats G – either metal, wooden or plastic tent cleats with three holes in each.

Knot one end of each guy rope, pass the rope through the upper hole of the cleat, through the eyelet in the sail, then back through the middle and lower holes in the cleat before tying it off to a snap hook which is connected to a screw eye in the corner of the seat slat. Repeat for the other three guy ropes (photo 5). Then add the mast ropes, running each one between the screw eyes at deck level via a screw eye in the top of the mast.

Sand all the edges carefully and then decorate the boat to taste using paint or wood stain.

5

4

A ROCKER THAT'S A TABLE TOO

Children always like toys that can be used in more than one way, and this simple yet clever design fills the bill perfectly: a rocker that turns into an all-in-one play table with two seats.

Materials

Use metric sizes for complete accuracy; imperial measurements are given as an *approximate* conversion.

From 12 mm (½ in) plywood
2 x 1 m x 600 mm (3 ft 3 in x 2 ft) A
2 x 670 mm x 370 mm (2 ft 2 in x 14½ in) B
2 x 670 mm x 250 mm (2 ft 2 in x 10 in) C
1 x 670 mm x 400 mm (2 ft 2 in x 10 in) D
Woodworking adhesive
Screws
Sandpaper

By painting the sides and ends as shown in the photographs, you can make the rocker look like a ship on one side and a car on the other – or anything else your children request. Best of all, it can of course be used inside or out of doors.

Making the rocker

1 Mark out the components carefully on the plywood sheet, making sure that the tongues and slots are accurately drawn. Cut each part out with a jig saw, then shape the side panels A and cut out the nine slots in each to the required dimensions after drilling a 12 mm (½ in) diameter hole at the end of each slot.

2 Insert the tongued ends of parts B, C and D into the slots in one part A, securing

Right: *Turned upside down and around, the boat becomes a desk, ideal for writing or coloring in the garden.*

Below: *This side has been painted to resemble a boat, and the whole structure rocks gently to add to the illusion.*

them with glue and with screws driven through A into the edges of the other parts. Repeat the process to attach the other part A. Weight or clamp the whole assembly until the adhesive has set to ensure strong joints.

3 Sand and round off all the cut edges carefully to remove any splinters. Then decorate the toy to taste using either paint or colored wood stains.

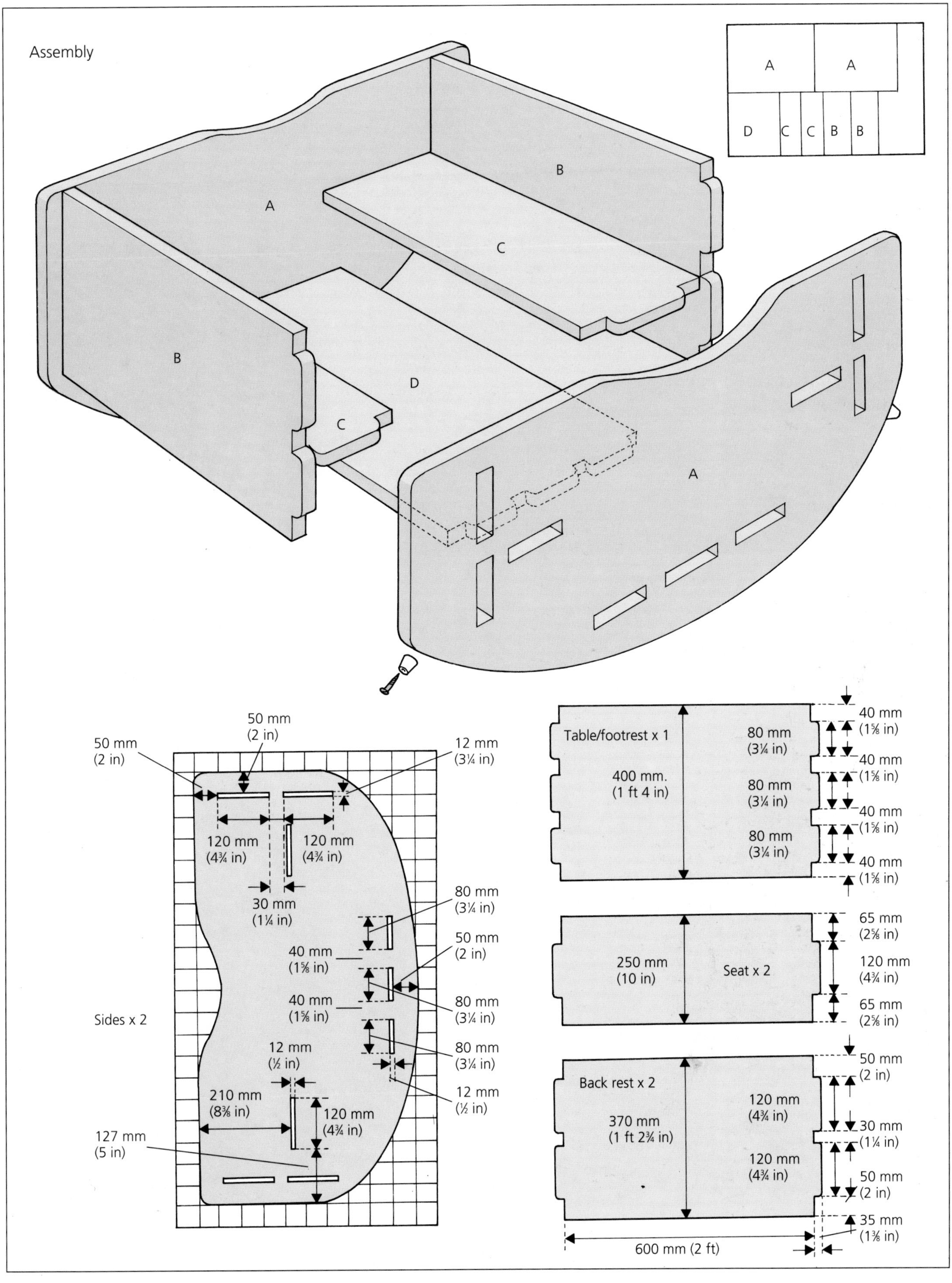

Assembly
A
A
D
C
C
B
B
A
B
C
B
D
C
A
50 mm
(2 in)
50 mm
(2 in)
12 mm
(3¼ in)
120 mm
(4¾ in)
120 mm
(4¾ in)
30 mm
(1¼ in)
80 mm
(3¼ in)
40 mm
(1⅝ in)
50 mm
(2 in)
40 mm
(1⅝ in)
80 mm
(3¼ in)
Sides x 2
80 mm
(3¼ in)
12 mm
(½ in)
12 mm
(½ in)
210 mm
(8⅜ in)
120 mm
(4¾ in)
127 mm
(5 in)
Table/footrest x 1
400 mm.
(1 ft 4 in)
80 mm
(3¼ in)
80 mm
(3¼ in)
80 mm
(3¼ in)
40 mm
(1⅝ in)
40 mm
(1⅝ in)
40 mm
(1⅝ in)
40 mm
(1⅝ in)
250 mm
(10 in)
Seat x 2
65 mm
(2⅝ in)
120 mm
(4¾ in)
65 mm
(2⅝ in)
Back rest x 2
370 mm
(1 ft 2¾ in)
120 mm
(4¾ in)
120 mm
(4¾ in)
50 mm
(2 in)
30 mm
(1¼ in)
50 mm
(2 in)
35 mm
(1⅜ in)
600 mm (2 ft)

A SOCCER GOAL

Soccer must be by far the most popular impromptu game in the world. All it needs is a ball and some goalposts. Why not make your own goals from some timbers, garden netting or canvas – plus half an hour of your time?

Above: *All kids love soccer, and if you have a patch of grass they will appreciate their own goal, and improve their game at the same time!*

Materials
1 x 1.5 m x 50 mm x 50 mm (5 ft x 2 in x 2 in) crossbar A

1 x 1.5 m x 50 mm x 50 mm (5 ft x 2 in x 2 in) base bar B
2 x 1.2 m x 50 mm x 50 mm (4 ft 2 in x 2 in x 2 in) posts C
2 x 900 mm x 50 mm x 50 mm (3 ft x 2 in x 2 in) side bars D
2 x 1.5m x 50 mm x 25 mm (5 ft x 2 in x 1 in) braces E
Screws

Plastic garden netting or shade cloth
Heavy-duty staples

Assembly

1 Cut all the components to length, Then join the posts C to the crossbar A with simple corner lap joints, screwed together. Repeat the process to join the side bars D to the base bar B.

2 Connect the posts to the side bars with lap joints to complete the basic framework. Then hold each brace E against the sides of the posts and side bars so you can mark the cutting angle on each end of the braces. Make the angled cuts and screw the braces in place.

3 Staple plastic garden netting or shade cloth to the back and sides and trim off any excess material all around.

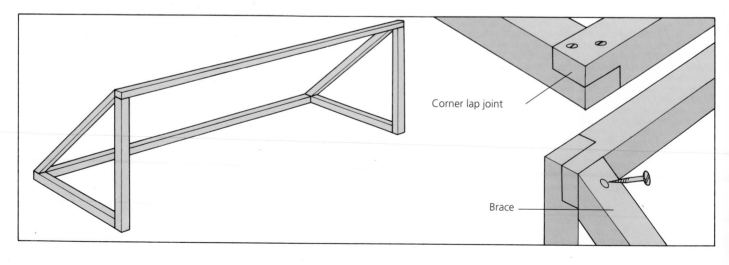

Corner lap joint

Brace

A SIMPLE TEPEE

When the children want to camp out, you can quickly rustle up a colorful tepee or two with some old fabric and three sturdy bamboo poles per tepee.

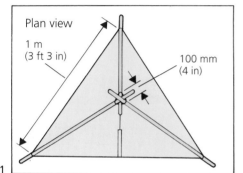

Plan view
1 m (3 ft 3 in)
100 mm (4 in)

1

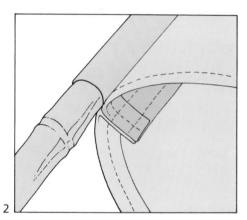

2

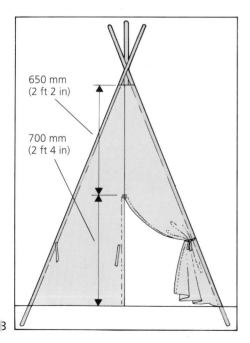

650 mm (2 ft 2 in)

700 mm (2 ft 4 in)

3

Materials
1 m (1 yd) wide fabric
Strong sewing thread
Tape
3 x bamboo poles

You can use any fabric so long as it is at least 1 m (36 in) wide; old curtains or sheets are ideal, and plain material can be decorated colorfully with fabric paints and stencils.

Assembly
1 Use a single piece of fabric for each of the two full sides and another – split up the center to form the opening – for the front. Each triangle should be about 1 m (3 ft) wide at the base and about 1.35 m (4 ft 6 in) high, with the apex of the triangle cut off squarely. Hem each piece all around.

2 Make up three tubes of fabric from 100 mm (4 in) wide strips of fabric, folded double, and sew the tubes and the edges of the triangular panels together (diagram 2).

Above: *This simple tepee can be made by anyone in just an hour or two.*

3 Sew strips of tape to the flap edges and the front fabric tubes to form ties to hold the flap closed or open (diagram 3).Then overstitch the top of the flap opening for extra strength (diagram 4).

4 Push the bamboo poles into the fabric tubes and poke their feet into the ground so the fabric is pulled taut. Tie the poles together at the top with wire or tape.

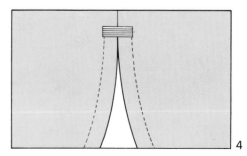

4

A WEATHER STATION

Make this portable weather station as an educational project for your children. It is designed to have a good flow of air by using louver panels which form the basic cabinet.

This is not so much a play project as an educational one, encouraging your children to take an interest in something that is all around them: the weather. This simple weather station is a portable box with a weatherproof roof and is fitted with open louvered walls and door to ensure a free flow of air round the instruments inside.

It is designed to house the three instruments that are most commonly used for recording changes in the weather: a minimum/maximum thermometer, a barometer and a hygrometer (also known as a wet-and-dry-bulb thermometer). The minimum/maximum thermometer records the highest and lowest temperatures that occur during the observation period, while the hygrometer measures the degree of humidity in the air. The barometer records changes in air pressure. Making daily visits to check the instruments can become an absorbing hobby, with everyone in the family trying to be a better weather forecaster than the professionals on radio and television!

Materials
4 x louver panels
Rails
Quadrant beading
Square beading
Plywood for base
4 x thin plywood
Woodworking adhesive
Screws
Panel pins
Carrying handle
2 x small hinges
Door catch
Mountings for inside

Assembly

1 Size the cabinet according to the sizes of the equipment it will be containing. Make up the four louver panels that form the walls and door of the cabinet. Each is a simple rectangular frame with butt joints at the corners, and the individual louvers are simply glued and tacked in position between the uprights (diagram 1).

Below: *Site your weather station where the air can pass around it freely and where you can easily see to take your readings.*

3

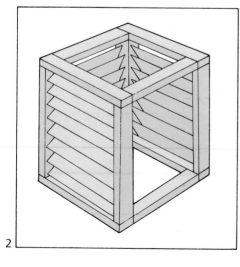

1

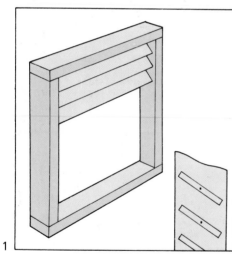

2

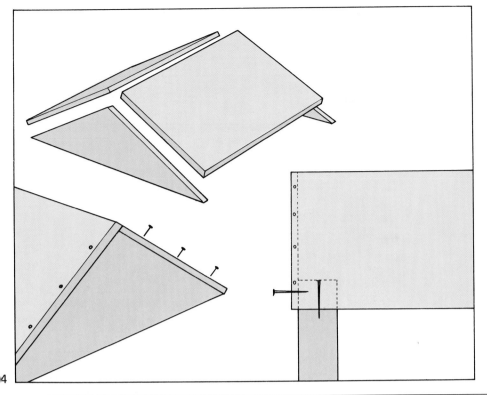

2 Glue and screw the wall panels together, then add top and bottom rails to form a frame for the door (diagram 2). Cut a piece of plywood to form the base of the cabinet, tack lengths of slim quadrant beading to the inner faces of the four bottom rails and glue it on top of them (diagram 3).

3 Make up the roof from four pieces of thin plywood, gluing and tacking the rectangular top sections to the edges of the gables. Tack and glue square beading to the tops of the short side walls of the cabinet, then screw the gables to these (diagram 4). Attach a carrying handle to the roof before securing it to the cabinet.

4 Hang the louvered door on two small hinges and fit a simple catch.

5 Finally, add mountings within the cabinet to hold the instruments. You may need nothing more complex than a cross-bar fitted with small hooks to hang the thermometers from, plus a shaped wooden block on which to sit the barometer.

4

A BASKETBALL NET

This final project is perhaps the simplest of all to make, involving little more than a panel of board, some stiff wire and some plastic netting, yet it will provide many hours of fun for adults and children alike.

Materials
1 x 900 mm x 750 mm (3 ft x 2 ft 6 in) MDO board, particleboard or plywood

White emulsion paint
Colored adhesive tape
Strong wire
Garden netting
Heavy duty staples

Making the board and net
1 Paint the board white, then mark a square on it with colored self-adhesive tape to outline the target area.

2 To make the net support, form the wire into a circle with a diameter about 50 mm (2 in) greater than the diameter of the ball the children will be using, leaving two straight 'tails' about 75 mm (3 in) long at the point where you close the circle. Then simply thread on the net 'skirt' at this

Above: *Tell your children that even commercial baskets are not for swinging on.*

point.
3 Next, drill two holes through the board at the bottom of the target square, push the ends of the net support through and then bend the wires down so they touch the rear face of the board. Secure them to it with staples.

4 Finally, mount the board on an outside wall well away from windows.
The standard net height is 3.05 m (10 ft), but if you are making this for small children, set it about 1 m (about 3 ft)

Staples

Sticky tape

GLOSSARY

Aggregate or concrete Fine stones (gravel) mixed with sand and cement. Combined aggregate is mixed sand and gravel.

Batten A slim strip of wood used to support clapboards and the like.

Blockboard A man-made board formed by gluing plywood plies to both faces of a softwood core. Exterior-grade board is essential if used for outdoor play structures.

Clamp A device with movable jaws used to hold components together during assembly.

Clapboarding Sawed or split boards used to cover the outside of a building. One of a series of boards with one edge thicker than the other, overlapped to cover the walls of a structure.

Clout nail or roofing nail A galvanized nail with a large flat head, mainly used to fasten sheet roofing materials.

Coach bolt or carriage bolt A long, round-headed bolt with a plain shank threaded at the end to accept a nut, used to bolt wooden frameworks together.

Deck, decking A wood-surfaced outdoor platform, often built on posts as a raised structure with a perimeter handrail.

Fencing board Sawed boards, often tapered in profile, used as covering for fences and outbuildings.

Fiberboard See medium-density fiberboard.

Fillet A batten with a triangular cross-section, often used at roof edges.

Hardcore Broken stone (gravel) used to consolidate soft subsoil beneath paths, patios and foundations.

Hardwood Wood from deciduous trees – those that shed their leaves in autumn.

Medium-density fiberboard or MDO A man-made constructional board formed by bonding wood fibres together with resins. Exterior grade board is essential if used for outdoor play structures.

Microporous paint or ranch paint A paint that allows moisture vapor to pass through the paint film from below; also available as varnish and wood stain.

Particle board A man-made constructional board formed by binding wood chips together with resin. Exterior-grade board is essential if used for outdoor play structures.

Plywood A man-made constructional board formed by bonding together several thin plies of wood. Exterior grade board is essential if plywood is used for outdoor play structures.

Post A vertical support for a structure, usually set in the ground and secured with concrete for stability.

Preservative A solvent- or water-borne chemical used to protect wood from rot.

Rail Any main horizontal element of a framed structure, supporting a floor deck or wall clapboarding or acting as a perimeter guard.

Skew-nailing or toe-nailing A method of nailing components together by driving the nails in at various opposing angles.

Softwood Wood from coniferous or evergreen trees.

Trellis A panel of open latticework fastened to a supporting framework and used for privacy and supporting climbing plants.

Wendy house A small play house for children, named after a character in J M Barrie's Peter Pan.

CHOOSING WOOD

For most of the projects featured in this book you will probably be using the most economical wood available in your area. This is likely to be a softwood such as pine, larch, or spruce. Some species, such as redwood and cedar, are naturally resistant to rot and insect attack, but others need preservative treatment for outdoor use. Most pressure-treated wood is impregnated with inorganic arsenic to protect it against damage by insects and fungi. Although some argue that this wood is safe after a period of time, others recommend against using it on surfaces that children may touch. Instead of using pressure-treated wood, you may choose to treat natural soft- or hardwoods with copper napthenate or sodium borate, which help prevent insect damage, and a water repellent, to keep wood from absorbing water.

If you want to use a hardwood you are likely to have a far bigger choice that will include temperate species such as oak, beech and ash. Compare prices with those for local softwoods before making your choice.

TIMBER SIZES

Standard sizes for sawed and planed (dressed) timber vary from country to country. For many of the projects featured in this book, the timber sizes are not critical; in these cases, use the measurements given as a minimum size guideline. In some cases where precise cross-sections are specified, using timber of a slightly different size will not affect the way the project is assembled. In a few cases, changing the timber size would affect other dimensions of the structure; in these cases, plane or rip the next available stock size down to the dimensions required.

INDEX